32 SHOR

Footbridge over the River Lin near Ulverscroft Mill.

32
SHORT CIRCULAR WALKS

Based on the Leicestershire Round

DEVISED BY THE LEICESTERSHIRE FOOTPATH ASSOCIATION

as a Millennium celebration

CORDEE – LEICESTER

Copyright: © Heather MacDermid for
Leicestershire Footpath Association 2000

IBSN 1 871890 39 X

British Library Cataloguing in Publication Data
A catalogue record for this book is available from the British Library

We hope this guide will enable and encourage people to enjoy walking
the footpaths of Leicestershire. Although every effort has been made
to keep the guide as clear and accurate as possible, we are sorry that
we cannot take any responsibility for your walks, so please take care.

All trade enquiries to:
CORDEE, 3a De Montfort Street, Leicester LE1 7HD

PREFACE

The walks in this book are based on the Leicestershire Round Long Distance path. They are intended for those who enjoy walking and feel they would like to sample the Long Distance walk, without the challenge of attempting the full 100 miles.

The Leicestershire Round was first devised and written by Leicestershire Footpath Association, to celebrate our centenary in 1987. The one hundred miles (for one hundred years) encircle the city of Leicester in a big sweep going through places of interest in beautiful countryside from the rugged rocky area of Charnwood, through the wide river valleys of the Wreake and the Soar up to the high and windy ridges of East Leicestershire and Rutland.

It goes across land where the Iron Age people chose to build their hill fort at Burrough Hill and then descends to lower slopes where many small streams feed the rich clay, arable fields. The route goes over the low hills of the Langtons with views over the wide Welland valley and gradually swings west to reach Foxton's famous staircase of locks before moving uphill over to wooded hills of Laughton, Gumley and Saddington. The route to the Roman centre of England, where Watling Street crossed the Fosse Way, is an easy and flattish route and the grassy Fosse Way usually makes for pleasant, trouble-free walking.

Northwards towards Bosworth Field where King Richard lost his crown and his life, the route joins the canal for a short distance and passes through the historic market town of Bosworth and the village of Shackerstone with its impressive 12th century castle mound. From there the land once more rises and you pass over former mining country to reach the outskirts of Charnwood at Thornton and Markfield and thence back to Newtown Linford where the walk begins and ends.

It has now become a well used route, signposted and maintained by the Leicestershire County Council and marked on OS maps. It has become popular as a challenge walk for ramblers of all kinds, and has been used as a sponsored walk for various charities. Many people walk short stretches of the way, confident that they are on a well marked and waymarked route. We hope that these short circular walks will in time be equally popular and equally well maintained.

For this book, the editorial team selected sections of the Leicestershire Round and mapped return routes to make pleasant, easy, interesting circular walks. These routes were walked by volunteer members of our association, who then wrote up the 'return to base' sections. Other members have 'foolproofed' the script as a final check.

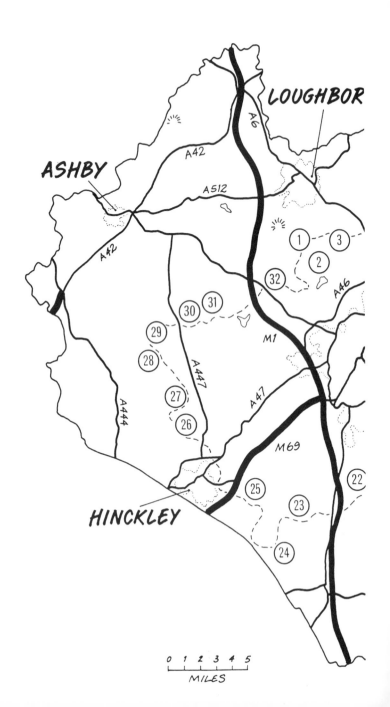

LOUGHBOR

ASHBY

HINCKLEY

A6

A42

A512

A42

A46

A44

① ③
②
③②
③⓪ ③①
②⑨
②⑧
②⑦
②⑥
A447
M1
A47
M69
②⑤
②③
②②
②④

0 1 2 3 4 5
MILES

6

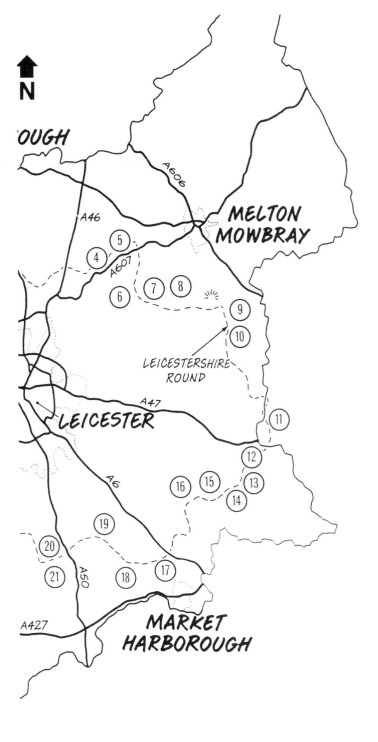

N

OUGH

A606

A46

MELTON
MOWBRAY

⑤

④ A607

⑦ ⑧

⑥

⑨

⑩

LEICESTERSHIRE
ROUND

A47

LEICESTER

⑪

⑫

A6

⑯ ⑮ ⑬

⑭

⑲

⑳

⑰

㉑ A50 ⑱

A427

MARKET
HARBOROUGH

The walks give the flavour of the varied countryside of Leicestershire. The paths go over land which is mainly agricultural. You need to respect the needs of the farming community and keep closely to the narrow paths of rights of way (single file or, at the most, two abreast) in cultivated fields. You need to follow the instructions accurately. The fields of Leicestershire are not an easy option for those wishing to walk at speed!

We have taken great care to make our instructions as clear as possible. But please note that however accurate our instructions and our maps at the time of writing, changes in the landscape do occur. You will need to be aware that hedges are still being uprooted, landmark trees do die, waymark signs do get vandalised, electric fences go up, new farm buildings appear, housing estates are built on farmland and new roads are constructed. A good walker is awake to such changes and ready to read maps and guide books with an eye to possible amendments.

Enjoy your walks in the new millenium!

Heather MacDermid,
hon sec LFA

Editorial team:
Heather MacDermid
Jim Mason
Steve Westby
Diana Davidson
Brian Jenkinson

ACKNOWLEDGEMENTS

Photos   Peter King

Maps   Jeff Nightingale

Foolproofing: Sandy Blades • Diana Davidson • Ray Dunkley • Jean Farmer • Clive Fennell • Colin Hames • Glenys Hargreaves • Mary Hodgkin • Ruth Ivens • Kate Jones • John Jackson • Eric Marchant • Syd Marsden • Jim Mason • Gillian Smith • Betty and Ted Spencer • Terry Stevens

GENERAL NOTES

BUSLINE 0116 251 1411 At the moment it is not easy to get to many of these little villages by public transport but we give the phone number in case you are able to find any services available for you.

CAR PARKING: 'Roadside parking' means parking with due consideration for others. Note that gateways should not be blocked, space by the church may be needed for services, for weddings or funerals, and local villagers may want the area by their shop left clear.

MAPS: We have used Pathfinder maps (Ordnance Survey 1:25000, 2 and a half inches to the mile, 4cms to 1km) though we expect Explorer maps to supersede them soon. These cover twice the area of pathfinder maps, at the same scale. Ask your map supplier for equivalent Explorer maps to the Pathfinders we recommend.

TIME: We usually suggest that an average walker does two miles in an hour, allowing for stiles or other obstacles and a short break for picnics! But you can take as long as you wish. Our members would perhaps do one of these walks in a morning and then have a pub lunch before doing another. You might choose to do one in an afternoon or a summer evening.

DISTANCES: We have used mileage and measured short distances in yards or paces.

LEICESTERSHIRE ROUND sections are printed in italics.

CONTENTS

Old John Tower from Hunt's Hill.

Autumn in Swithland Woods.

HUNTS HILL
Woodhouse Eaves   Hunts Hill

1

How to get there Hunts Hill car park is at the foot of Old John, the beer mug shaped monument in Bradgate Park, two miles by road from Newtown Linford. You could walk through the park from Newtown Linford to reach it. This would add on a couple of very pleasant miles.

Car parking Hunts Hill, Swithland Woods for a small charge, and in Woodhouse Eaves (free). Toilets are available in these car parks.

Public transport Regular bus services to Newtown Linford and to Woodhouse Eaves. Ring Busline.

Map Pathfinder 874 (SK51) Loughborough (South).

Route A lovely all year round walk which includes Swithland Woods and Bradgate Park.

Mileage 4 miles approx.

Refreshments Various inns, restaurants and shops in Woodhouse Eaves. Ice cream vans in Hunts Hill car park. Picnic tables in Swithland Woods.

Items of interest Swithland Woods are an excellent place to spot flowers, trees, birds and rocks.
Woodhouse Eaves church stands on a rock cave.

The walk *From Hunts Hill car park, cross the road and continue towards Shepshed on the road opposite (B5330 Benscliffe Road).*
Turn right, and cross the stile into the second field, to walk close to the hedge on your right. The route goes to the bottom left corner of the field, past a spinney over to your left. (But the farmer usually leaves a good headland for people who wish to walk round the edge of the field to reach this point.) Cross through the stiled field corner and walk with the hedge on your left across the Lingdale golf course, to reach the road (Joe Moore's Lane).

Cross the road carefully to continue in the same direction beside the golf course, close to the hedge on your right. The route across the golf course is usually well signed. In the corner of the field, beside the fairway, pass the rocky outcrop of Spring Hill Wood on your right. You need to keep in the same direction, but make a detour right, along an old line of trees and then after 50 yards bear left round a small copse of trees. Keep the hedge on your left until you come to the stile and slate bridge which takes you into the corner of a field, with Maplewell farm in the far left corner.

A view over the blue waters of the quarry pool in Swithland Woods.

N

Church

Victoria Rd.

Maplewell Rd.

Maplewell Fm.

WOODHOUSE EAVES

Brand Hill Road

gravel track

'The Wheatsheaf'

Fm.

Swithland

Joe Moore's Lane

Spring Hill Wood

golf course

Swithland Wood

Benscliffe Rd. B5330

slate quarry

Hunt's Hill

car park

START

MILES

0   1

The path continues to the corner of the field just to the right of Maplewell farm buildings, though you are expected to move round the edges of the field, to your right, to reach this point. Pass under the telegraph wires and cross the stile. Follow the faint track, with the hedge on your left. Keep in the same direction, joining the gravel track from Barn Farm.

This bends left to meet Maplewell Road, where you turn right to walk downhill into Woodhouse Eaves.

From Maplewell Road, Woodhouse Eaves turn into Victoria Road and walk up the steep hill to the top of the road. Turn left and follow the track which runs between houses and gardens. This brings you out onto Brand Hill Road, near the church.

Turn right. Pass The Wheatsheaf pub (Real Ale!) on your right. Turn right at the T-junction and walk towards Swithland. Turn right at the footpath sign just before the first house on your right (by the 30mph sign). Cross the stile and follow the path to the next stile and information board. Keep in the same direction, ignoring the path to your left. When you meet a path coming in from your right, bear left following bridleway marker posts.

The path soon widens and goes through a grassy picnic site before narrowing to a forest path again. Follow it to reach a T-junction with a wooden fence on your right. Turn right and follow the wooden fence now on your left, skirting round the old water filled slate quarry. At the junction of paths continue straight ahead to reach a small clearing, complete with litter bin.

Turn left and follow the path up and over the hill. Keep straight on the main track which bends right to cross the wooden plank bridge over the little stream. Take the narrower path to the right and wind your way between trees until you come to an opening in the boundary wall. Cross the road and take the footpath signposted to Old John, which stands very grandly ahead of you. Cross the stiles and go through the kissing gate into Bradgate Park.

Here you have a choice! Turn right and follow the boundary wall and go through the next kissing gate, back to Hunts Hill car park or make your way up to Old John, to admire the views and then descend to this kissing gate and return to Hunts Hill car park, where the walk began.

David and Valerie Joyce: "Take binoculars and pocket book identification guides for this lovely walk."

WOODHOUSE EAVES
Broombriggs   Beacon hill   Woodhouse Eaves   **2**

How to get there Woodhouse Eaves is on the B591 road and well signposted from Quorn, Rothley and Anstey.

Car parking There is a public car park in the centre of Woodhouse Eaves on Main Street next to the village hall. This walk could also be started at either Upper or Lower Beacon car parks. (Pay and display machines and notice boards with clearly displayed locking up times.) All three car parks have public conveniences.

Public transport Reasonably frequent buses to Woodhouse Eaves. Ring Busline.

Map Pathfinder 874 (SK51) Loughborough (South).

Route One of the highlights of the Leicestershire Round! Easy tracks in a popular area of Charnwood. There are many possible routes over Broombriggs and Beacon Hill, all well used and well waymarked (but not with the distinctive Leicestershire Round waymarks.) You can choose whichever suits your style and the time available.

Mileage about 5 miles.

Refreshments available in Woodhouse Eaves. Ice cream vans usually parked at the Beacon car parks.

Items of interest Woodhouse Eaves has a church built on a rock. The windmill which stood on Windmill Hill was destroyed in the 1940s. Only the base now remains.

Broombriggs Farm was given to the County Council in 1970. The farm trail notice boards give interesting information about farming, and the views from the top are magnificent

Beacon Hill was bought for the public in 1946. It was formerly owned by the Beaumanor Estate.

The walk *From Maplewell Road, Woodhouse Eaves, take the wide grassy path beside house number 100. Turn left through the bridle gate and then immediately right to walk on the well used path, close to the hedge on your right. Pass, over to your left, the wooded knoll of Round Stye spinney, and walk towards Long Stye spinney, the wood which goes up the hill ahead to your left. When you reach the foot of Long Stye spinney turn left and follow the farm trail, going steeply uphill, close to the stone wall of Long Stye wood on your right. The view from the top is worth the climb! You can look back to Windmill Hill and*

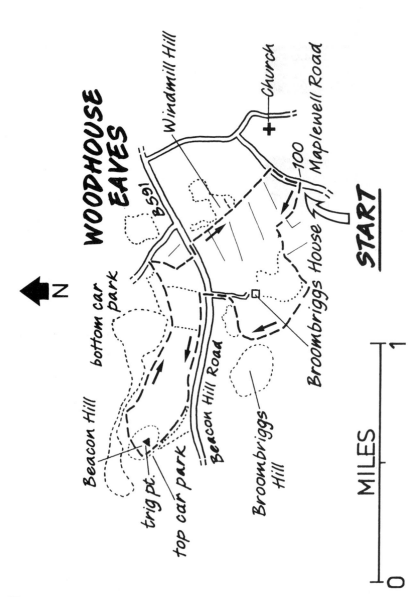

Looking over Woodhouse Eaves at the quarried rape of Buddon Wood, from Broombriggs.

beyond to Quorn and the Soar Valley. Go through the little triangular walled enclosure into the picnic site field, where you have views over the other side of the hill, eastwards over to Copt Oak and Ulverscroft.

At the end of Long Stye spinney keep in the same direction and cross the stile, beyond the farm gates. Move towards the wall over to your left, but do not cross it. (Beyond the field wall lies the farm of Upper Broombriggs). Go uphill to the little clump of trees, (a walled enclosure of holly and beech, beside a waymarked seat), in the top left corner of the field. Cross the stile and continue gradually uphill close to the enclosure wall on your left. You are now at the top of Broombriggs Hill, 200 metres above sea level, with Broombriggs House down to your right. Keep close to the fenced off bracken and gorse and make a big semicircular sweep around Broombriggs House, going gradually downhill with the plantation wall on your left. Continue on the wide fenced-off grass sward and meet the wide, walled drive from Broombriggs House.

Continue down the drive to meet Beacon Road (B591). (Woodhouse Eaves lies to your right.) Cross carefully and keep in the same direction, through the belt of woodland. Meet the main track up to Beacon Hill. Turn left and walk uphill to the highest point.

At the top of Beacon Hill pass the white trig. point and the toposcope over to your right. Continue on the main track. It circles the highest point and then descends gradually down to the Lower Beacon car park.

Just before you reach the car park turn right on the waymarked path which crosses an open grassy area. Look for an unmarked path on your left, between trees. This leads you out onto Beacon Hill Road, a little lower than where you first crossed it. Turn left and cross the road by the Broombriggs Farm Trail sign.

Go through the car park and follow the hard track which leads through a handgate to a small wooded area. (Here you can if you wish turn left and climb Windmill Hill, to see the base of the old mill. The path swings round and brings you back to the main track a little further on.)

Follow the track to meet Maplewell Road. Turn left to reach the centre of Woodhouse Eaves.

David and Valerie Joyce: " Binoculars and a pocket identification book would be useful for those who are bird, tree and flower enthusiasts. Broombriggs Farm Trail has a number of useful information boards. You can pause to read Board 5 on Land Quality and Use, Board 6 on Grasses and Board 8 on Hay and Sileage."

The craggy summit of Beacon Hill, Leicestershire's second highest point.

WOODHOUSE EAVES
Rabbits Bridge   Quorn   Old Woodhouse

3

How to get there Woodhouse Eaves is on the B591 road and well signposted from Quorn, Rothley and Anstey.

Car parking Woodhouse Eaves and Quorn have public car parks.

Public transport Regular bus service. Ring Busline.

Map Pathfinder 874 (SK51) Loughborough (South).

Route Easy walking on level tracks (but beware the muddy bit by the old railway bridge!).

Mileage 3 or 4 miles.

Refreshment Numerous pubs in Quorn and in Woodhouse Eaves

Items of interest Interesting and varied buildings in Woodhouse Eaves, including the church built over a cave in the rock and a new round Baptist chapel.

Old Woodhouse has a fine row of old almshouses built by Mrs Perry Herrick for her workers.

From Rabbits Bridge you can walk a little way to have a fine view of Swithland reservoir.

The walk *From the bottom of Maplewell Road cross the road junction and continue along Meadow Road. The road continues as a grass track, to the right of the primary school. After a few yards along the track, cross the stile on your right and go diagonally right on a well walked path to meet a hedge corner. Walk with this hedge on your right to meet the road. Cross straight over the road and follow the headland with the hedge on your left. You are going to continue in this direction for five fields, passing the tall silos of Rushey Fields Farm, uphill to your right, and heading towards Buddon Hill. Cross the two concrete farm tracks and continue close to the hedge on your left.*

(The Great Central railway line lies between you and Buddon Hill. The path, which formerly led straight to the ancient settlement on Buddon Hill, is deflected by the railway and now swings right to meet the railway crossing at Rabbits Bridge.)

At the end of the fifth field move to your right and keep close to the hedge on your left. From the stile in the corner of the next field you need to cross an open field. Pass close to the isolated oak tree and continue towards the railway line, passing a small water treatment building.

Windmill Hill from the Broombriggs trail.

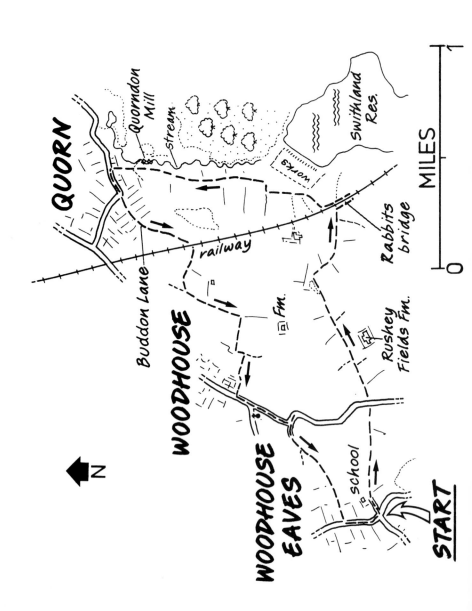

The Great Central Railway near Rabbits Bridge.

Cross the concrete cartbridge and turn right, to walk uphill close to the railway line. Meet the lane and turn left to cross Rabbits Bridge, pausing to wave at steam trains passing below.

Leave the bridge by going down the embankment on the left hand side. Pass through a small wooded area over a footbridge and follow the broad grassy track swinging right and then left. Cross the footbridge with cast iron railings. To your right you can catch a glimpse of the grounds of Swithland water works.

Follow the well trodden path along a shady lane and a field (usually cropped). Turn right, over the stile, and walk between a fence on your left and the meandering river on your right.

This section can be very muddy in wet weather.

Cross the stile ahead and join the hard track. At the road Quorn village centre lies to your right but our route continues by turning left. Walk along the road. When the main road swings right do not follow it but continue straight ahead down Buddon Lane, which becomes a grassy track which goes through a spinney. (To avoid the wettest parts of the track make your way up to the higher path through the spinney.)

Pass through the railway tunnel and turn sharp right to enter an open field, close to a hedge on your left. At the top of the field turn left to walk along the hard track. Turn right at the T-junction and left at the next junction. (Note the lovely thatched cottage over to your left.)

Turn right onto a narrow road which takes you into the old village of Woodhouse.

At the main street, turn left. Fork left at the road junction. Pass Old Woodhouse church on your right.

At the bottom of the hill turn right into a small road leading to a footpath beside the stream on your left. Cross the open meadow and go through the kissing gate to continue on the path past the cricket field and children's playground. Meet the main street of Woodhouse Eaves, where the walk began.

Katrina Durant: 'Marcus and Sarra, who were still to be convinced of the pleasures of walking, found this "a very pretty walk every step of the way" '.

How to get there Rearsby is 7 miles from Leicester on the A607 Leicester-Melton Mowbray road. Follow the turn off to Rearsby.

Car parking Roadside parking only, with discretion. You may find space in Brookside, Rearsby

Public transport Regular bus service by Midland Fox XI, XIA. Ring Busline.

Map Pathfinder 875 (SK61) Melton Mowbray and Syston.

Route Mainly meadowland, with some crop fields. Pretty villages in the Wreake valley and fine views from the higher ridge between Brooksby and Rearsby.

Mileage 4 and a half miles.

Refreshments The Wheel and The Horse and Groom, Rearsby and The Blue Bell, Hoby all serve bar snacks.

Items of interest Brooksby, famous for its connections with the Villiers family George Villiers leapt to fame and power as the favourite of James I and of Charles I . He became the Duke of Buckingham and was reported to have possessed every vice and only one virtue (that of being generous to his mother, brothers and sisters!)

The Hall, once lived in by Lord Cardigan and Earl Beatty of the North Sea is now an agricultural college. (Little remains of the original building.)

The church is lovely, with early Tudor features. There are monuments in the church to William Villiers and his young wife who both died in 1711.

_____

The walk *From Rearsby church turn right at the top of Church Lane and follow the tarmac path which goes round two sides of the church wall to emerge on Church Leys Avenue. At number 22 turn left and go between houses, through the kissing gate and turn right in an open grassy area between the convent grounds and an avenue of chestnut trees.*

Pass the convent garden wall on your left and meet the road. Turn left to go downhill and cross the road to walk along Wreake Drive. At number 7 turn left. Cross the double stile into the open field and move diagonally right across the ridge and furrow to the railway crossing.

Cross the railway line carefully. Thrussington church tower lies straight ahead but our route goes diagonally right to reach Thrussington Mill.

27

A glimpse into the grounds of Swithland Water Works.

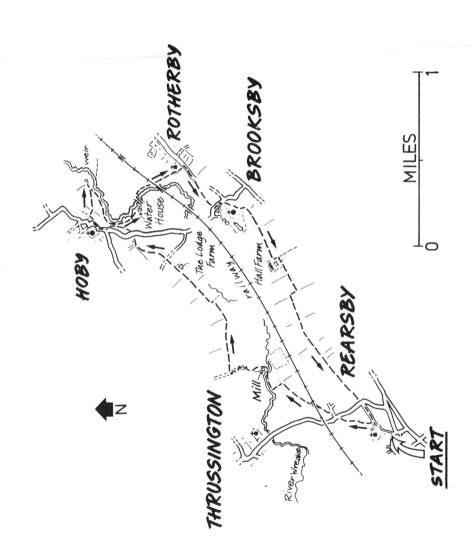

Leicestershire's 'Taj Mahal' in the Swithland Water Works.

Keep diagonally across two fields, but in the third turn left to follow the hedge on your left. (If the diagonal route is obstructed by crops you might find it easier to turn sharp right when you have crossed the railway and keep to the edge of the next two fields, keeping close to the railway at first and then turning sharp left to reach the stream.)

Walk to the river side and then turn right, to keep close to the river on your left. Cross the brick bridge over the river and walk with it on your right and the old mill lock on your left. Swing left over the metal footbridge and pass the mill house and garden on your left. Cross the concrete cartbridge beside the old mill wheel housing (the marks of the old wheel are just about visible on the wall). Pass between the outbuilding and the big sheds and continue along the mill access drive.

As you go along the drive, note Thrussington church tower to your left and Hoby church spire over to your right. When you are level with Thrussington church, turn right, into a field with huge pylon. Pass the pylon on your left and continue in the same direction across a very big field. Pass the end of one hedge and carry on to meet another in front of you. Keep this hedge on your left and continue with it on your left in the next two, long, fields. (You will be aiming for Brooksby church spire at this point and an arched brick bridge, which you pass but do not cross.) (The beautiful grounds over to your right are Brooksby Agricultural College grounds.)

Aim for the red brick house of The Lodge farm. Hoby church spire is clearly visible beyond it. Pass to the left of the house and follow the drive. Cross the road and continue straight across the open field. Move slightly left in the next two small fields. Pass an isolated house over to your left. Cross the cartbridge at the end of a line of trees and continue to the stile which leads you out onto the Brooksby-Hoby road ahead. Cross this road and swing left in the field, keeping the road on your left. Cross old gravel hollows and rejoin the road at a waymarked concrete post crossing. Continue uphill to the road junction and turn right, to pass Hoby church on your left.

From Hoby church take the metalled footpath next to the Village Hall and go between wall and houses to reach Back Lane.

Turn left then right to walk down a steep hill on narrow path. Cross the stile and bear left to reach the yellow marker post in the corner.

Here we part company with the Leicestershire Round and turn right along the river bank. Cross the footbridge and keeping the river on your left, pass through the gate and go along the river bank beside the Water House on your right.

Pestilence Cottage, Old Woodhouse.

Turn left to cross over the river bridge. Walk with the river now on your right. Rotherby church stands ahead of us. As the river bends away to the right, keep straight on towards the railway line. Cross it carefully and keep in the same direction heading towards Rotherby church. Pass it on your left and go through the gate onto the village street. Turn right.

Brooksby church is now straight ahead, along the road. Cross the cattle grid and bear right, away from the road and cross the field diagonally to the stile onto the Hoby Road. Turn left and walk along the road for a short distance and then turn right, into Brooksby Agricultural College. Continue along the drive following yellow markers through the college grounds. Swing left before you reach the church and follow the waymarks over the stile. Continue with a hedge on your right and keep in the same direction over the fields. Go through a series of waymarked gates to reach the farm road leading to Hall Farm. When you reach the farm buildings turn left and then right, following the track (signposted to Hives Farm) along the back of the farm buildings.

Keep on this track, which bends right and then left and, when the track turns left to Hives Farm (Equine Centre), keep straight on. Cross the stile at the top of the hill and go through the gate at the end of the field. The village of Rearsby is now in view. Keep close to the hedge on your left to the corner of the field and then move right to join a walkway leading to a metalled road in front of houses.

At the end of this road cross the main road and continue along Church Leys Avenue to reach Rearsby church. Follow the path which goes to the left of the church and at the church gates turn left again to reach the old packhorse bridge and the ford.

Di Chapman.

HOBY
Frisby   Gaddesby   Hoby   5

How to get there From Leicester take the A607 Melton road, through Syston, East Goscote. Pass Rearsby and in approx. 2 miles turn left on the minor road signposted to Brooksby Agricultural College. Follow this road for approx 1 mile to Hoby.

Car parking Street parking only. The road is quite wide near the church.

Public transport Limited. There are infrequent buses which pass near Brooksby and Gaddesby. Ring Busline for details.

FRISBY on the Wreake

HOBY

old Mill

railway

START

ROTHERBY

A607

Cross (rems)

f.b.

f.b.

Brooksby Hall

BROOKSBY

Nursery

N

Coles Lodge

Carlton Lodge Fm.

wood

F.b.

Rose Cottage

MILES

0   1

GADDESBY

The Seven Arch bridge, Rearsby.

Map Pathfinder 875 (SK61) Melton Mowbray and Syston.

Route Mainly fields, some farm tracks and some road. There is one steep(ish) climb out of Frisby to the main road but no other difficulties.

Mileage 8 miles. Allow approx. 4 hours

Refreshment Pubs at Hoby, Gaddesby and Frisby. The Bell, at Frisby, serves excellent food at moderate prices.

Items of interest Churches in Gaddesby, Brooksby and Rotherby. The River Wreake winds very prettily by Hoby and Brooksby.
Rotherby village has pretty houses, an interesting church, the city greenhouses, but no public facilities. The city greenhouses are sometimes open to the public.
Brooksby Agricultural College gardens are sometimes open to the public.

The walk *From Hoby you can turn right along Back Lane, opposite the church or continue past the church to reach the Blue Bell Inn. The footpath on your right just before you reach the pub takes you down a metalled track beside the village hall, between walls of houses to reach Back lane, where you turn left and then right.*

From Back Lane, Hoby, turn right when you reach the row of brick cottages and walk steeply downhill on the fenced-off path. Cross the footbridge over the stream and go diagonally left across the big field to meet the river in the corner of the field.
   A good spot for kingfishers!
Turn left and walk with the river on your right. Cross various now useless bridges. (This is the site of an old mill.) Swing right and cross the long, arched footbridge spanning the river by the old weir.

Keep in the same direction, aiming for the left of the houses of Rotherby, visible in the distance. Cross the footbridge. Go through the railway handgates and cross the line carefully. Continue in the same direction, close to the hedge on your right. In the top corner of the field cross the hedge and turn left. (Rotherby village is now behind you.)

Keep the hedge on your left for two fields. In the third field continue in the same direction, parallel with the hedge over to your right. Cross the stile (mind your head on the finger post!) by the road sign 'To Frisby 1 mile'.

Cross into the field on the opposite side of the road and walk close to the hedge on your right for three fields. The road moves away to the right but the footpath keeps in the same direction across pasture fields

The parish church of All Saints, Hoby.

with interesting humps and hollows. Frisby church spire comes into view. Go through a small rectangular field. Move slightly left towards the spinney, cross the stile and move slightly right to find the crossing directly 'under' the church spire! Follow the gravel drive to emerge on Water Lane, Frisby, near the old village cross. The Bell Inn lies opposite you.

(Frisby church, with its Norman tower, and the pretty village green lie to your left, along Church Lane. The village is worth a little detour. Several houses have 18th century dates. There is a general store and post office. The pub serves food.)

From Frisby pass the Bell Inn over to your left and walk along Rotherby Lane passing the old cross stump on your right. At the derestriction sign, turn left to cross the stile and go uphill close to the hedge on your left. (Look back to see Frisby with its fine church spire.) The hill flattens out and you meet the main A607 Melton-Leicester road, near the remains of a second old cross stump.

Continue in the same direction on the other side of the road. In front of you lie the bands of low hills which you cross to reach Gaddesby.
Go downhill at first, keeping parallel with a hedge over to your right. Pass close to a pond on your right and make for the jutting out corner of a field ahead. Continue with the hedge on your left. The next crossing is near a big tree. Move slightly right to cross the footbridge.

Go uphill over ridge and furrow pasture to the top right corner of the field and then downhill close to the hedge on your right. Cross the footbridge in the bottom right corner of the field and continue uphill to the top corner. Enter a big open field, with the sheds of Coles Lodge ahead, over to your left, and a small brick barn over to your right. Keep in the same direction, over the crest of the hill going between Coles Lodge and the brick barn. Cross the drive and go straight across the field and through the gap (near the large tree at the right of the line of trees in the hedge ahead). Continue downhill in the open field. The roof of Harborough Farm comes into view over to your left, in the valley below. Go through the waymarked gate, near a clump of trees and pond to the right of Harborough Farm.

Cross the valley, moving slightly right to the good footbridge. Move very slightly right to the next stile, half way along the hedge ahead. Continue moving slightly right to the far right corner of the next field, passing Rose Cottage, the imposing brick house in the trees, on your right.

Meet the road and turn right into Gaddesby.

If you wish to explore the very pretty village of Gaddesby, with its lovely church and hall and fine old brick houses and visit the pub you need to turn left and make a half mile detour and return refreshed to this point to continue the walk. (The Cheney Arms pub stands on the corner of Main Street and Rearsby Road.)

Take the Rotherby Lane which leads from Gaddesby village and continue in the same direction (due north) to reach Carlton Lodge Farm (half a mile).

Pass Carlton Lodge Farm on your right and turn left onto the Midshires Way bridlepath. This starts as a green lane which finishes just before the wood on your left and then becomes a well-defined track which bears right. Follow the track with the hedge on your left. When it turns right towards the farm, walk straight on, through the gate, with the hedge on the left to reach a handgate.

The main A607 road and the village of Rotherby with its tall slim church tower lies ahead. In the distance on a clear day you can see Ragdale Hall.

Carry on in the same direction. At the end of the field join a farm track which leads through the farm buildings and past a nursery. Meet the A607 Leicester-Melton road.

Cross this main road carefully, using the central refuge. Continue in the same direction down the lane signposted to Brooksby Agricultural College. The college stands in grounds on your left, where the parish church is open to visitors and well worth a visit.

Turn right along the gated road signposted to Rotherby. Turn left when you reach Rotherby church and follow the footpath with the church wall on your right. Keep in this direction to go downhill to cross the railway. TAKE CARE. FAST TRAINS PASS FREQUENTLY.

Now walk close to the River Wreake on your left and cross the brick, hump-backed bridge. Turn right immediately and go through the little gate which leads you onto the cobbled path in front of The Waterhouse.

When the stream bends right keep straight ahead to go uphill to the waymarked stile onto the road. Turn right and walk carefully along the road to reach Hoby church where the walk began.

Steve Westby.

GADDESBY
Ashby Folville   Barsby   Gaddesby

6

How to get there Gaddesby is midway between Leicester and Melton Mowbray. Leave the Leicester-Melton road at Rearsby, following signs to Gaddesby.

Car parking Park on Gaddesby, Main Street or, if you have permission, on the Cheney Arms pub car park.

Public transport Buses are very infrequent. Ring Busline.

Map Pathfinder 875 (SK61) Melton Mowbray and Syston.

Route This is a very easy walk, mostly pasture, all paths well used and clearly defined on the ground.

Mileage 4 miles.

Refreshment Cheney Arms pub at Gaddesby. The Carrington Arms at Ashby Folville has a very good reputation for food.

Items of interest In Gaddesby visit the church to see the Colonel Cheney monument. Note the date stones on Harewell cottages, Harewell House and, less obvious, Morton House.

In Barsby we pass a small building known as Tower House or Godson's Folly, which resembles a church and stands on Church Lane. It may never have been consecrated as a church and is now simply a dwelling. More date stones to inspect, much older this time: 1701 in brick on The Cottage, 1691 next door at Stoneleigh and opposite, 1701.

The walk From the Cheney Arms, Gaddesby, towards Rearsby and then turn right into Chapel Lane, passing Cross Street on your right. Take the signposted footpath along a track towards Firs Farm and after just ten yards turn right over a stile into a narrow field. Bear left after a second stile and plank bridge. Turn right and follow the hedge on your right. Turn right after another stile into a tree nursery and continue to the road. Take Pasture Lane opposite and, immediately after the last house, turn right over a stile onto the Leicestershire Round. Follow this field edge path along the back of houses to two stiles crossing a drive which leads to Hall Farm

---

Move diagonally left, going downhill to cross the corner of the field. Aim for the clump of tall trees on the horizon. Cross the footbridge and go over the stile on your left in the corner of the next field. Continue in the same direction, uphill, making for the left side of the clump of trees. These trees actually border the stream, on a sharp meander below the hill.

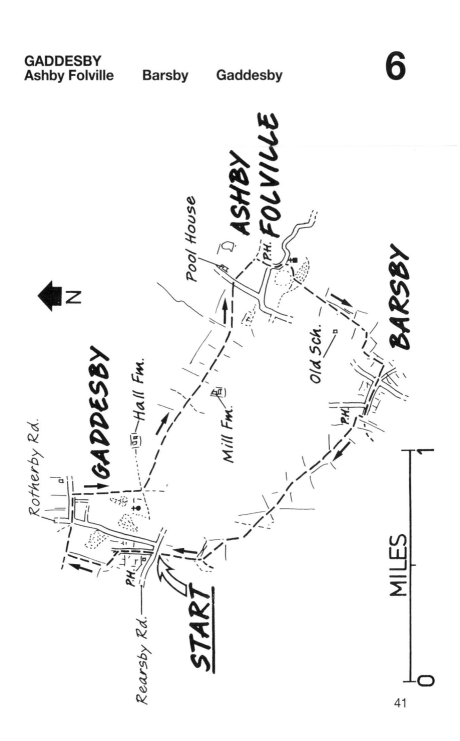

Monument to Edward Cheney a veteran of Waterloo, Gaddesby Church.

Continue down to the bottom left corner of the field. The well waymarked route now follows the valley, past the disused windmill base of Mill Farm and the stream over to your right.

Keep in this direction, crossing the fenced-off Midshires Way bridle-track and make for the stile in the corner of the field, near the stream, slightly to your right. Cross the open field and meet a hedge on your right. Keep in the same direction, and then move slightly left to pass a sewage works which is over to your right. Continue moving left uphill to reach the far left corner of the big field, near Pool House on the lovely tree-lined road from Ashby Folville to Great Dalby.

Cross this road and move slightly right in the field, away from the hedge on your left. A line of houses lies ahead, with Ashby Folville church tower over to the right of them, in the trees. Cross the stile half way along the line of houses and emerge on Highfield End, by a steep flight of brick steps.

Turn right and go down Highfield End, Ashby Folville. Bear left along the road in front of The Carrington Arms and village hall, both overlooking the village cricket field. Turn right into Church Lane and right again onto a footpath in front of Brook Cottage. Cross two bridges, a small paddock and the Manor House drive. Continue in the same direction through parkland pasture, with stiles 5 or 10 yards from the fence on your left.

The isolated house over to your right was formerly a school serving Ashby Folville and Barsby, being convenient for neither village! The hedge steps in close on your left and you pass through a narrow field. In the next, much bigger, field the path crosses to the centre of the far hedge. Leave the field by a handgate onto a hedge-lined path.

Enter Barsby by a small, brick towered building (Godson's Folly). Turn right through the village and follow Main Street. When the main street of Barsby turns right, take The Lane at the left of the now boarded up, (1999) King William public house. Turn right onto a footpath track then cross the stile into fields. Bear slightly right, looking for a pond by the hedge and a well hidden stile just beyond.

As you climb the stile, note the fine view of Gaddesby church, much better from here than in the village it serves. Bear left across this field and after another stile, head for the far left corner. Continue across two more fields with poorly defined stiles, using as a sight-line the farm complex with the poplar trees. Turn right after the ditch crossing and follow the field edge to a clump of trees. Cross into the next field and turn half left across the field towards the double gabled house. Cross the footbridge and follow the track back to the Cheney Arms, Gaddesby, where the walk began.

Ken Brockway

ASHBY FOLVILLE
Thorpe Satchville   Twyford   Ashvy Folville

7

How to get there From Leicester take the A607 towards Melton. Turn right in Rearsby on B674 through Gaddesby to Ashby Folville

Car parking Ashby Folville pub car park is for customers only. You need to check when the gates will be closed. There is plenty of space on Highfield End (the dead-end road next to the pub) but be considerate of other users. There is some space near the Church but the little road is busy.

Public transport Bus 100 goes to Ashby Folville. Ring Busline for time-tables.

Map Pathfinder 875 (SK71) Melton Mowbray and Syston.

Route This lovely walk starts at the pretty village of Ashby Folville near a good pub. It begins with an easy section of the Leicestershire Round through interesting countryside to the village of Thorpe Satchville. The return route is on a bridleway and easy to follow footpaths, with great views. Some fields will be sown with crops, but the route is likely to be quite easy to follow in spite of the crops, since they are well signed and well used. There are no difficult stiles to cross.

Mileage Just 4 and a half miles.

Refreshment Two pubs on route. The Carrington Arms in Ashby Folville is a very popular pub, serving good beer and food. The Fox Inn at Thorpe Satchville now provides a warm welcome for walkers.

Items of interest Beautiful Leicestershire! Hills and fields, a pleasant meandering stream (Gaddesby Brook), two pretty villages and a lovely church in Ashby Folville. The map shows some old fish ponds next to the Manor House, and the whole village of Ashby Folville has a feeling of still being part of a Manor, with its long tree-lined drive heading towards the pub, and impressive wide "tile topped" brick wall round the Manor, and dramatically big houses. We pass the lovely Church and the converted stables which must have been part of Folville Manor at some time. Major Smith-Carrington leads walks round the village from time to time. The V.S.C.C Vintage car meetings are held at The

The Carrington Arms, Ashby Folville.

ASHBY FOLVILLE
Thorpe Satchville   Twyford   Ashby Folville

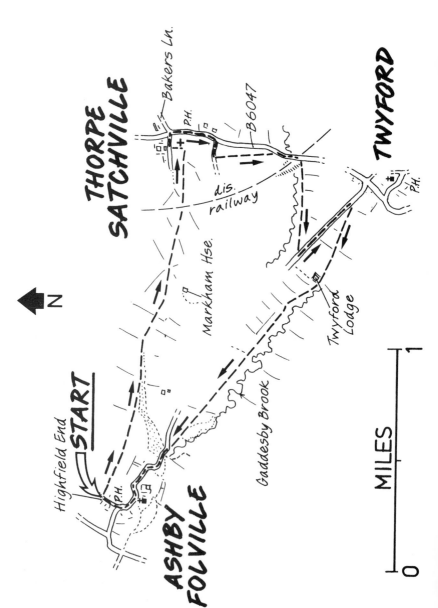

Carrington Arms on the second Tuesday in the month, when you can expect cars to the value of several million pounds to be parked in the car park, in the road, and in an adjacent field . Last time we went, there was a newly built Buggati in the car park on which a cool £250,000 had just been spent.

The walk *From Ashby Folville church make your way (west) to the Carrington Arms pub. Turn right up Highfield End for 200m. Turn right at the Leicestershire Round signpost. Walk slightly uphill close to the hedge of the white house on your left and keep in the same direction. Follow the groove down the middle of the field to a big tree. (Ashby Folville is now over to your right, in its woodland setting.)*

Keep in the same direction across the big open fields, with the tree-lined stream over to your right. Pass close to the waymarked telegraph pole in the middle of the field and continue to the huge electricity pylon ahead. Pass an isolated house over to your right (Markham House) and make your way up to the far left corner of this open field. The houses of Thorpe Satchville come into view on the hill ahead. Continue in the same direction, across the little corner of one field and into the corner of a very large field, bordered ahead by the hedge of the tree-lined railway line. Keep moving diagonally left to cross under the tall arched brick bridge of the dismantled railway. (From the high ground of this field you get fine views.)

Continue across the little corner of the field and continue steeply uphill to Thorpe Satchville, moving gradually away from the hedge on your left. (The hall is in parkland beyond this hedge.) Pass close to big farm barns on your left and cross the waymarked stile in the top corner of the field. The little bell tower of Thorpe Satchville church comes into view. Swing left around the ha ha wall of the large house and garden on your left and turn left across the stile into the churchyard.

Pass the little church of St Michael and meet Church Road. Turn right to meet the main A6047 Melton-Market Harborough Road, opposite Bakers Lane, Thorpe Satchville. Here we leave the Leicestershire Round.

Turn right and follow the road, towards Twyford, passing The Fox pub on your left. At the end of the houses, just before the road bend, turn right, down a lane. Go through the gate with weight restriction signs. After 20 yards turn left where the left hand hedge ends. Head for a gap in the trees with a shed on the right. Go through the gate and follow the waymark sign over the next large field. Admire the views and aim for the bottom left corner where the old railway meets the main road. Cross the stile and turn right, along the road for 20 paces. Turn right at the bridleway sign and almost immediately turn left to go through a gate. Follow the signs ahead through three gates. After the third gate head across the large field keeping close to the hedge on your right to reach the bottom left corner of the field.

Meet the road and turn left for about a quarter of a mile. Just before the houses turn right into a gateway. Cross the stile and turn right again. Walk diagonally to the far corner of the field, passing a large barn and a new building to your right. Cross the next five fields by the waymarked stiles, meeting a stream on your left and passing Twyford Lodge (a large barn, with a partly built farmhouse and a caravan) on your right. Cross the track and the stile near the large hawthorn tree. Make for the field corner.

Follow the left hedge of the field near the meandering brook. Cross the stile and follow the waymark pointing ahead, to the right of a large pylon. From the pylon, make for the waymark post ahead. (The stream meanders left then rejoins the path). Go through the gate to another waymark post on the right of a small wood. Cross the footbridge into a big field where the next waymark can be seen at the far edge of the field. Cross the stile and move slightly right to skirt the edge of the next wood. From the corner of the wood make for the road sign, which shows above the hedge. When close to the road sign follow the hedge left for a short distance. Go through the gate, where our route crosses the Midshires Way and turn right to meet the road. Go left to follow the road back to Ashby Folville church and the pub.

John Cutting: "A really nice circular route on fairly well used paths with good gates/ stiles, well signposted and no problem crops or barbed wire and no nettles or in sight (in August)."

THORPE SATCHVILLE
Burrough Hill   Burrough on the Hill

8

How to get there A47 towards Uppingham through Houghton on the Hill. Turn left to Tilton and follow the B6047 to Twyford and Thorpe Satchville.

Car parking Street parking only. Try Bakers Lane where the verge is quite wide beyond the houses.

Public transport Ring Busline.

Map Pathfinder 875 (SK71) Melton Mowbray and Syston.

Route Quiet road, track, pasture. The route between Burrough on the Hill village and Thorpe Satchville is usually ploughed. There are some

THORPE SATCHVILLE
Burrough Hill   Burrough on the Hill

8

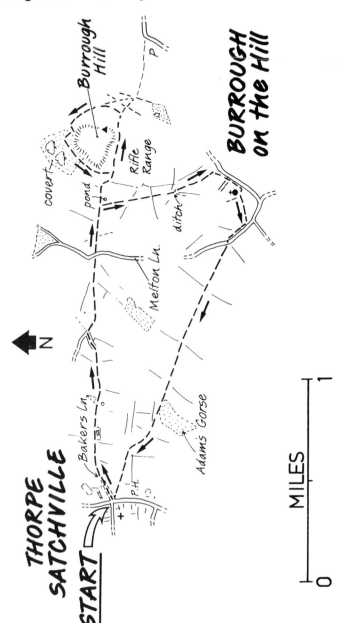

MILES

49

quite steep inclines. (This is hilly countryside!) We follow part of the Dalby Hills Permissive Path to encircle Burrough Hill.

Mileage About 5 miles.

Refreshment Pubs in Thorpe Satchville and Burrough on the Hill.

Items of interest Burrough Hill Iron Age encampment. Land open to the public and owned and leased by the LCC. The notice board gives the historical information. 700' above sea level deserted in early part of Roman occupation. Whit games were held here in the 16th century and horse races in the late 19th century. The toposcope indicates places within view from this high point.

The walk *From Thorpe Satchville crossroads follow Bakers Lane for about a mile. At the cross roads of paths, where Bakers Lane goes sharp left, turn off right, through a gateway and down the steep track of Salters Hill. The route to Burrough Hill can be seen ahead of you extending as a well marked track up to the ramparts above the steep escarpment of the Iron Age hill fort. Follow the track down to the Melton Lane. Cross this road carefully and continue along the field road up to Burrough Hill. The track bends right in the top corner of the field to cross through two hand gates.*

Follow the track which takes you up past the Iron Age hill camp on your left. (The toposcope stands high up on the ramparts. To see it you can choose whether to go left up the steep hill or continue in more sedate fashion along the main track, going gradually uphill and then swinging left to enter the hill fort by the main entrance gap in the ramparts. It is worth the walk across the wide open spaces to reach the toposcope and look around you, but our walk continues from this entrance. From the toposcope make your way to the trig. point by the main entrance and go through the gap in the ramparts.)

The main track to the car park lies ahead. The information board stands in the fenced enclosure and the car park with picnic tables and toilets lies further along the track. (If you go there return to this point.) From the information board we turn away from the track and walk in the open pasture field with the ramparts and trig. point on our left and a hedge over to our right. Follow the waymarked route (of the Dalby Hills Permissive Path) parallel with the ramparts and gradually downhill through a gorsey narrow way.

When the path forks go left towards the farm gate half way up the hill. Look for a stile to the left of this gate, a little higher up the hill. Cross this and follow a little path through the wood (open to the public).

Heavy going on the approach to Buttermilk Spinney, Burrough on the Hill.

Fork right to descend a steep little bit of path and continue through the very pretty mixed woodland. Go through a good handgate at the end of the wood. Continue along the contour of the hill with ramparts high up on your left. Pass the sandy rabbit bank edge and go gradually downhill, swinging right to rejoin the Leicestershire Round path by the gates you met earlier.

Go through the two gates and follow the edge of the field on a good track, retracing your earlier steps to reach the clump of hawthorns which encircle a pond. This is your marker for your route to Burrough on the Hill village. Turn left. (This path should be marked and cleared as it is an old County Road, once visible as a good track, but for many years the path has not been reinstated, as it ought to be. Help mark the path with your footsteps in a good single file track! We hope the route will eventually be waymarked.)

Pass the hawthorn-edged pond on your right. Cross the huge ploughed field, aiming for two huge isolated trees ahead. The gap to cross is to the left of the trees. You are now in line with Burrough on the Hill church spire. As you approach the hedge ahead move slightly left and go through the wide gap between two large ash trees.

Continue towards the spire, parallel with a conifer plantation uphill over to your left. Go through a farm gate and cross the nettle patch, jumping the ditch if it is wet. In the next field turn left and go through the gap into the corner of a big field. Burrough on the Hill village can be seen diagonally up right. Go up across the field to reach a hedged lane, to the left of the church spire. Go uphill on a good grassy track between hedges. Meet the road and turn right into Burrough on the Hill. (Beware of traffic!)

As you enter Burrough on the Hill village pass the church graveyard and turn right to go through a gate towards the church. Bear left and cross the stile by a wall. Walk diagonally left to cross a stile in the left hand corner of the field. Continue diagonally left past the corner of a garden and cross the stile to the right of a bungalow.

Meet the road and turn right. When the road swings right, look for an opening on the left into the corner of a field. Walk along a track, close to the hedge on your right. When the track bends left, continue straight on. Just before the corner of the field, turn right, through a gap and then immediately left to cross a wooden bridge and through another gap, to walk with the hedge on your left.

At the end of the field pass through a gap to the right of the corner. Cross a plank footbridge and walk up the field bearing slightly left. Cross the stile and continue slightly right, from Adams Gorse wood.

Cross a stile, plank bridge and stile and walk up the field towards the hedge on your right. Go over the brow of the hill and aim for the bottom right corner of the field. Cross a plank bridge and stile and walk uphill bearing diagonally right towards the hedge on your right.

At the top of the hill go over the double stile in the hedge on your right. Turn left to walk with the hedge on your left. Ignore the metal gate and cross the stile in the corner. In the next field bear diagonally right to a stile halfway along the hedge in front of you. Cross the stile and continue diagonally right towards Thorpe Satchville village hall and the main road through the village, where the walk began.

Steve Westby

Our foolproofers say:
"These instructions are wonderfully clear and the walk is delightful, especially the circuit of Burrough Hill BUT the bit from Burrough on the Hill village to Thorpe Satchville needs a health warning: not to be undertaken lightly in bad weather!"

SOMERBY
Burrough on the Hill   Somerby

9

How to get there Somerby lies in the triangle formed by Leicester, Melton Mowbray and Oakham and is easily reached from any direction by car. From Leicester take the A47 towards Uppingham. Turn left along B6047 through Tilton to Twyford. Turn right through Burrough on the Hill to Somerby. From Melton take the A606 towards Oakham. Turn right at signs to Pickwell and Somerby.

Car parking There is no public car park but parking is usually possible on the main street if you use care and consideration. There is a Pay and Display car park at Burrough Hill, where it is possible to start the walk.

Public transport Minimal. It might be possible with care to use bus services for this walk. But check with Busline.

Map Pathfinder 875 (SK71) Melton Mowbray and Syston.

Route One very steep hill and one very muddy section of path (on the Dalby Hills permissive path). Lovely views and pretty villages.

Mileage 5 miles.

NB. Please note that the Dalby Hills permissive path is occasionally closed by the Ernest Cook trustees on Thursdays in the shooting

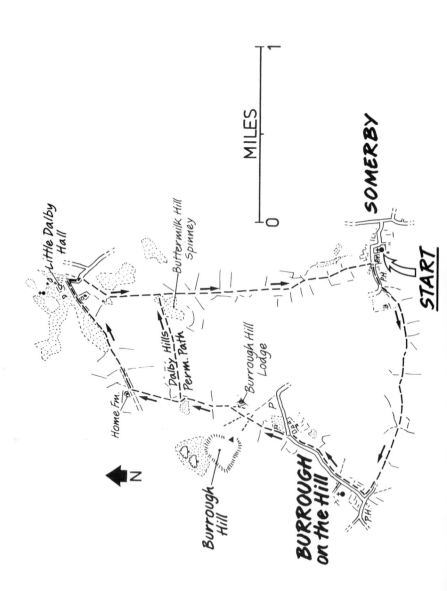

season. You might need to make a detour by going further downhill to walk along the road. This adds a mile and a half to the route. A notice board informs you when the path is closed.

Refreshment There are two good public houses in Somerby, both serving a wide range of bar snacks and more substantial meals. There is also a pub at Burrough on the Hill.

Items of interest Burrough Hill the Iron Age hill fort. The notice board gives you the historical information. It is now a popular place for flying model aircraft and kites.

There are marvellous views from the top of these hills.

The walk From Somerby church walk along the High Street, passing two pubs on your left. At the far end of the village, where the road bends sharp right, go half left along an avenue lined with horse chestnut trees. Beyond the avenue continue along the minor road which bears slightly right. Where the road turns slightly left, turn right to follow the footpath sign.

The footpath follows the parish boundary hedge on your left. Go through the farm gate, where panoramic views of the county open up to the south and west, with Burrough on the Hill in the near distance ahead. A beautiful valley shaped by the sculptured contours appear below you on the right.

Continue in the same direction to a waymark post a short distance ahead and then bear slightly right, downhill, making for a waymark post near where the hedge in the valley on the right converges towards a line of trees.

Cross the footbridge and keep in the same direction to reach the next hedge and then bear slightly right towards a corner of wire mesh fencing. Continue with this fencing on your right. Join the access road and go uphill. Turn right at the minor road and pass Burrough House on your left.

Meet the Somerby Road and turn right for half a mile. (No pavements. Take care.) Turn left at the footpath sign by a clump of conifers and walk along the track past the underground reservoir. Keep the hedge on your right at first but cross the double stile half way along this hedge and continue in the same direction but with the hedge now on your left. Meet the access drive to Burrough Hill. Our route continues from this point, but you can turn right to make a short detour to the toilets and car park picnic site or turn left for a close look at Burrough Hill, the Iron Age earthwork.

To continue the walk, cross the track and keep in the same direction. *Burrough Hill Lodge is over to your right. Cross the waymarked stile to the left of the house and turn left to walk close to the hedge on your right. Go through the bridle gate in the top corner and keep in the same direction to go over the crest of the hill in a big open field. The next crossing is by a little corner of the field, where the hedge projects a bit. Go steeply downhill to meet the track leading to the Dalby Hills permissive path.*

The notice board on your right informs you whether the permissive path is open or not. If the path is open, follow it for half a mile to the next notice board at Buttermilk Spinney, where you turn right. Ignore the next two paragraphs.

If the permissive path is closed you will need to go downhill from the notice board. Go through the bridle gate and follow the bridleway across the field. (It should be clearly visible even if the field is ploughed.) Meet the Dalby road just to the right of Home Farm. Turn right and walk along the road towards Little Dalby. (You will be able to see, on your right, the track which leads up to Buttermilk Spinney, but you need to take a semicircular detour along the road to reach the public footpath to it.) Continue along the road towards Little Dalby. (Ignore the lane on your left.) The road bends sharp right and you soon need to turn right, on the footpath signposted to Somerby.

Cross down to the bottom left corner of the field, between two spinneys. Cross the footbridge and make your way up the fenced-off path. Meet the farm track and turn left to Buttermilk Spinney. Pass the Ernest Cook Trust notice board on your right.

Both routes now continue from Buttermilk Spinney into the Punch Bowl. (Gird your loins: there is a steep climb!) Continue straight ahead up to the top of the ridge. (Ignore the permissive path, which goes off to the left, along the valley.)

From the top of the ridge there are fine views. The spire of Somerby can be seen ahead. Aim for a point slightly right of the spire and keep in this direction, (due south). The fields are usually ploughed and not reinstated but there should be a discernible line of footprints to show you the way across the dip of the second open field and up to a waymarked corner. Walk with the hedge on your right in the next field. When the hedge ends, continue in the same direction across the open field.

On the ridge over to your left Pickwell church tower should be visible. Ahead of you lies a wooded hollow, with a stream, crossed by concrete planks. This is a very pretty area, home to many wet meadowland wild flowers. You need to go straight ahead to reach the footbridge, but to avoid the wettest ground, move slightly right to pass the spring.

The next waymarked stile leads you up into the corner of the field, close to the hedge on your left. Move slightly right at the field corner to cross into a small corner of rough ground. Continue close to the hedge on your left in the next field. Cross the track (which leads to the sewage treatment plant on your left) and continue in the same direction, through the group of trees to follow a line of big trees which leads you into a jitty between houses on the main street of Somerby opposite Manor Lane.

Somerby church lies to your left. The Stilton Cheese Inn lies to your right and The Old Brewery to your left.

Arthur Hopson: "The walk is quite strenuous as this is hilly countryside. It passes through mixed farmland providing beautiful views."

SOMERBY
Owston   Somerby

10

How to get there Somerby lies in the triangle formed by Leicester, Melton Mowbray and Oakham and is easily reached from any direction by car.

Car parking There is no public car park but parking is usually possible on the main street if you use care and consideration.

Public transport There is only a limited bus service available from Melton Mowbray. No service on Sundays.

Map Pathfinder 875 (SK71) Melton Mowbray and 895 (SK70) Leicester (East) and Houghton on the Hill.

Route A very pleasant walk through rolling hill farm and pasture land of east Leicestershire, a landscape of small grass fields and low hills, well waymarked, with no difficult stiles.

Mileage 5 miles.

Refreshment There are two good public houses in Somerby, both serving a wide range of bar snacks and more substantial meals.

Items of interest Somerby village is full of interest. There are beautiful ironstone houses and an impressive rectory and a lovely church

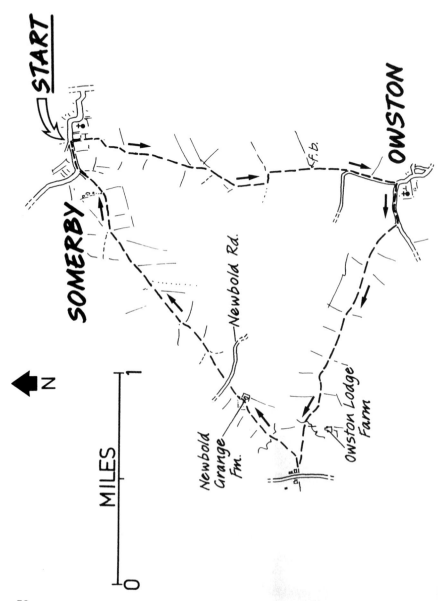

Looking towards John O Gaunt from near Tilton on the Hill.

with an interesting graveyard. (Look for the stone of Dr Benjamin Richardson, famous for the speed of his operations, in the days before anaesthetics when this was a vital factor.)

Owston is a tiny hamlet, once the site of an important Augustinian abbey founded in 1161. The evidence remains as humps and hollows in the fields near the church.

The walk *From Somerby, by the pubs, walk along Manor Lane. A gate at the end leads into a long, narrow field. Keep close to the hedge on your right and go through the gate to the right of the telegraph pole. The hedge is now on your left. Go downhill for three fields. At the end of the third field the stream comes in from the left. After 100 yards, turn left and cross the footbridge over the stream. Go up the bank and turn right to walk with the stream down to your right.*

Go through the gateway ahead, where the spire of Tilton can be seen on the hill ahead. Turn left to walk uphill with hedge on your left.

At the next gate a diversion sign indicates that you should turn left to reach the edge of the field and then right to walk downhill close to the hedge on your left in this field and the next. The gate onto the road is just to the right of the bottom corner. Turn left and walk along the road into Owston.

On entering the village of Owston, turn immediately right along the road signposted to Marefield. Ignore the footpath sign on your right and continue along the narrow lane until the road rises ahead after about 300 yards. Turn right onto a gravel bridlepath, keeping the hedge on your right as the path rises ahead.

The spire of Somerby church can be seen immediately to the right across the rolling landscape.

Go through one large field and pass a recently built farmhouse on your left. Continue uphill through a gateway and keep the hedge on your right. Go downhill to a gate and cartbridge and continue uphill, still with the hedge on your right.

The path now crosses a track (leading to Newbold Farm on your right). After about 300 yards go through the hedge, so that you walk with it on your left. Owston Lodge Farm lies ahead but we turn right before we reach it. At the bottom of the dip follow the waymark sign, going through the gate on the right and then heading diagonally left to cross a small bridge and go through a gate. Continue uphill through a series of single wired enclosures, keeping the hedge on your right.

Before reaching White House Farm ahead, turn right at the waymark,

The Elizabethan Launde Abbey and Park.

go through the metal gate and walk downhill with the hedge on your left towards Newbold Grange Farm.

The path now goes downhill to cross a substantial brick-faced footbridge over the stream and continues uphill keeping close to the fence on your left. Go through the gate and follow the signs, with the hedge now on your right.

At the farm buildings the path is diverted to take you right and then left. Watch out for the waymark sign at the end of barns on your left, as it can be easily missed. The path does not go straight ahead, but changes to the left side of the hedge and runs alongside the main driveway, an avenue of trees.

The path now crosses a country road and continues in the same general direction. Ahead of you the path switches from left to right of the hedge and shortly back again to pass through a gate. Once through the gate you need to leave the hedge over to your right and move slightly left to reach a clearly waymarked gate. The path is clearly visible ahead, as it rises through the fields.

The village of Burrough can now be seen on the skyline to your left.

The path again switches to the right. Continue with the hedge on your left until you reach a wire fence. Go through the gate and follow the path which runs diagonally across the last two fields to join the road back to Somerby to your left.

The spire of Somerby comes into view ahead of you to your right. Enter the village via the lovely avenue of horse chestnut trees.

Neville Townsend: "It is likely that you can complete the walk without seeing another person."

BELTON
Leigh Lodge   with optional loop via Withcote   **11**

How to get there From the A47 Leicester to Uppingham road two parallel roads lead into Belton. They are linked by Main Street and meet at the church. The church stands on a corner, opposite the stone cross at the junction with Chapel Street.

Car parking No public parking space but some of the village streets are quite wide. Park with discretion. Nether Street is quite wide.

BELTON
Leigh Lodge

with optional loop via Withcote

11

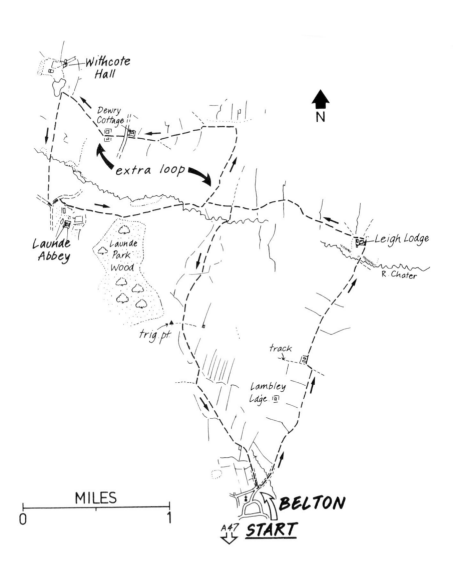

Withcote Hall

Dewry Cottage

extra loop

N

Launde Abbey

Launde Park Wood

Leigh Lodge

R. Chater

trig pt

track

Lambley Ldge

MILES

0   1

BELTON START

A47

Public transport Ring Busline.

Map Pathfinder maps 895 (SK60/70) Leicester (East) and Explorer 15 (Rutland Water and Stamford).

Route Hilly, with lovely views over wooded countryside. Mixed sheep pasture and arable land. The Leicestershire Round section goes beside the little River Chater and then up and over the Ridlington Ridge on farm tracks which are sometimes very muddy. There are spectacular views. Rutland Water and the Eyebrook reservoir can be seen from the top of the ridge.

Mileage 5 miles (ADD ON the 4 mile loop to WITHCOTE to make a longer walk)

Refreshment Belton, The Sun Inn on Main Street and tea room. Village shop near the church.

Items of interest Launde Abbey chapel, sometimes open to the public.
Withcote, a lovely redundant church with old glass.
Belton a pretty village.
Leigh Lodge, with its old fishponds, the site of a hunting lodge in the forest in the time of King John.

The walk From Belton church pass the war memorial on your right and continue left down Chapel Street. At the fork take the road to the right, signposted to Lambley Lodge, No Through Road (and waymarked as the Leighfield Way). When the lane turns left to Lambley Lodge, continue straight ahead with the hedge on your left.

At the top of the hill turn left along a wide track until you reach a big barn, where you turn right at the bridleway sign. Go downhill on the ashphalted drive. Cross the bridge over the River Chater and follow the drive past Leigh Lodge on your left. Ignore the bridleway which turns right. Pass close to the conservatory and indoor swimming pool of Leigh Lodge.

Ignore the footpath which goes off diagonally right and continue on the farm track ahead. At the T-junction of tracks keep straight ahead and cross the open field, moving towards the hedge on your right. At the end of the field pass a waymarker and walk between two lines of barbed wire. Cross a bridge over the stream and continue up the slope and through a gap in the hedge. Keep in the same direction, heading for a large gap in the hedge ahead. In the next field walk with the hedge on your right. Meet a track.

To return to Belton on the 5 mile walk, turn left on the track and omit the next section.

Optional extra loop (4 miles)
Continue for a short distance on the track, passing a farm track on your right and then turn right to walk uphill through a new plantation of trees close to the hedge on your left. At the top of the hill turn left at the T-junction of paths and follow the hedge on your right. At the end of the field ignore the bridleway which goes off to the left but continue straight on with the hedge still on your right. At the end of the field turn left. Pass one waymarked opening and continue to the next. Go through the metal gate and walk downhill with the hedge on your left, heading towards some sheds. Go through the metal gate in the bottom corner of the field, passing to the left of the sheds.

Meet the track and turn right towards Cottage Farm and Dowry Cottage. Pass the cottage on your right and cross the road. Follow the drive to Avenue Farm. Pass the farmhouse on your right and swing slightly right to follow the splendid avenue of trees. When you reach the big barn at the end of the avenue, turn left to join the Leicestershire Round.

Make your way past the isolated big barn and turn left . Walk close to fencing on your right and join a well-defined track close to Withcote lake on your right. Once past the barn, move uphill, away from the lake. The path to Launde Abbey goes over the hill (just to the right of the brow) and down to a footbridge over the River Chater at the point where the telegraph wires cross the stream.

Cross the footbridge and go up the gulley. At the top of the rise you should see Abbey Farm ahead. Veer slightly left as you cross the big pasture, to meet the road which can be seen coming steeply downhill to Launde Abbey. The chimneys of Launde Abbey come into view and then you see the whole building. Turn left at the cattle grid just before the road junctions. (For a closer look at the beautiful house you need to cross the grid.)

Turn along the road towards Withcote for a short distance and then turn right along the well-marked bridleway between the abbey and the lake. Go through the gate and continue up the slope. (On your left is the restored entrance to the Abbey's 'ice house'.)

The path leads you, parallel with a railing fence over to your right, towards the corner of Launde Park Wood. Go through the gate to the left of this corner and continue diagonally across the big field to the far left corner. Go through the gate and cross the bridge over the little river Chater. Keep to the right in the next field along a fairly well marked path, with the river on your right. Go through the wide gap in the hedge and then follow the path as it swings left. Go up the slope and follow the hedge on your right, passing a new plantation on your left. HERE YOU REJOIN THE SHORT WALK by turning right on the wide farm track.

THE SHORT WALK Follow this track all the way up to the top of the hill. From the top you can look left along the Ridlington ridge and perhaps catch a glimpse of Rutland Water. Go through the bridle gate in front of you, where views open up ahead towards the Eyebrook reservoir.

Keep the hedge on your right at first as you descend the hill then follow the green track down to the bottom left corner of the field and continue with the hedge on your left until you reach the road, near the big brick house, Brickle Farm.

Turn left along the road and walk for a mile into Belton. Chapel Street leads you to the memorial cross and the church and the general shop. The Sun pub is a little further down the hill, on Main Street.

Steve Westby: The extra loop is worth the effort.

ALLEXTON
Fearn Farm   Horninghold   Allexton

12

How to get there The A47 Leicester-Uppingham road passes between Belton and Allexton.

Car parking There is very little space for cars at Allexton. It would be wiser to park beside the road into Belton and to risk life and limb crossing the wide, fast and furious A47 Leicester-Uppingham road to reach Allexton church and the green beyond it.

Public transport Ring Busline for details of the bus service. Alight at the Allexton-Belton junction.

Map Explorer Map 15 (Rutland Water and Stamford).

Route Ups and downs, with good views across open country.

Mileage 6 miles.

Refreshment The Sun Inn at Belton for light refreshment. You may also find food and drink, by arrangement, at Fearn Farm.
(The owners serve light refreshments and provide camping space. Advance warning is a useful precaution. Tel. 01858 555285)

Items of interest Allexton church is now disused but has a fine late Norman interior and two extraordinary Victorian dormer windows in the roof.

ALLEXTON
Fearn Farm   Horninghold   Allexton

12

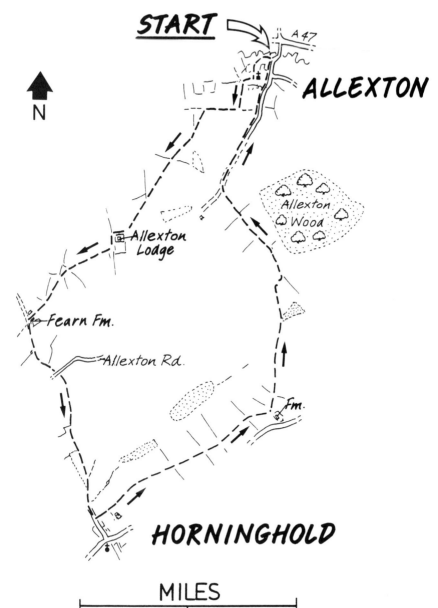

START

A 47

ALLEXTON

N

Allexton Wood

Allexton Lodge

Fearn Fm.

Allexton Rd.

Fm.

HORNINGHOLD

MILES

0   1

67

The duck pond, Hallaton.

Horninghold has an interesting, mainly 13th century church and a street of large and well kept houses built about 100 years ago as a model village.

The walk *From the green in Allexton, with the church to your left and the gates to Allexton Hall on your right, go up the lane between houses. The lane becomes a green track between hedges and is waymarked with the Leicestershire Round logo.*

At the end of the track enter an open field and turn right to follow a bridleway. Allexton parkland is on your right. When you are level with the hall, on your right, swing left and walk uphill, following the telegraph lines. Cross the waymarked stile in the fence on your right, half way up the hill.

You now aim for Allexton Lodge, on the hill ahead, crossing the corners of three big ploughed fields. Just before you reach Allexton Lodge, at the foot of a rough pasture, turn right along the (recently diverted) path. Follow the wire fencing on your left and turn uphill to pass Allexton Lodge.

Turn right at the first hedge past the house. (You are now back on the old route.) Pass under the telegraph wires, and walk downhill, close to the hedge on your left. Go through the gate and keep in the same direction across the little corner of the field. As you go over the rise ahead you should see Fearn Farm, your next target, on top of the hill, on the far side of the valley. The stile is just to the right of the farm barns. At the lane turn left to pass Fearn Farm.

Here we leave the Leicestershire Round. From Fearn Farm follow the lane downhill to meet the Hallaton-Allexton road. Go straight across the road and through the metal double gate. Keep in the same direction. Large farm buildings come into view ahead. Follow the hedgerow on your left and pass through the next iron gate. Keep close to the hedge and go through heavy double gates. The hedge is now on your right and the path becomes a metalled track into Horninghold.

Our path turns left before we reach the houses but the village is well worth a visit. The church is usually unlocked. If you explore, return to this point.

From Horninghold follow the footpath sign which points between wire fences, beside mature horse-chestnut trees, with the impressive stable block buildings over to your right. Cross the stile and follow the irregular hedge on your right to reach the stile.

You now follow waymarks and a succession of stiles, keeping along the crest of an ascending ridge towards Muckleburgh Farm. (The fields may be ploughed but the path should be cleared.) In the first field pass a pond and a spinney. In the second field pass a fenced pond. Muckleburgh Farm becomes visible straight ahead. Cross the stile to the left of this house and then swing left (due north) on a grassy track. (This is an old County Road, waymarked with a red sign.) Go through two iron gates and keep close to the hedge on your right to go through the next, wooden, gate and the gate at the near end of a narrow strip of woodland. Continue in the same direction across the next, open field, aiming for a hedge with two prominent trees.

Go between the two old gate posts and follow the pleasant, easy lane. This soon becomes a metalled track which leads onto the Hallaton-Allexton road. Turn and walk along this quiet road to Allexton, where the walk began. (Or continue straight ahead to cross the A47 if you parked at Belton.)

Syd Marsden: "The route is some 6 miles, but owing to the undulating nature of the ground, feels longer!"

HALLATON
Horninghold   Fearn Farm   Hallaton   13

How to get there A6 south to Kibworth. Turn left at Kibworth and follow signs to Hallaton.

Car parking No public car parks but street parking is not difficult. Use discretion.

Public transport to Hallaton very infrequent (two buses per week!). Ring Busline.

Map Pathfinder 916 (SP79) Wigston and Kibworth Beauchamp.

Route A walk through the wide open spaces of east Leicestershire with good views and two interesting villages. The hills are mainly downhill!

Mileage 3 and a half miles

Refreshment Pubs at Hallaton. The Fox Inn stands by the village duck pond. The Bewicke Arms is by the village green. Both pubs serve refreshments. Light refreshments at Fearn Farm by arrangement (tel. 01858 555285).

Items of interest Hallaton, one of Leicestershire's prettiest villages is worth a leisurely stop. The High Street leads past the old conical butter

The conical market cross, opposite the Bewicke Arms Hallaton.

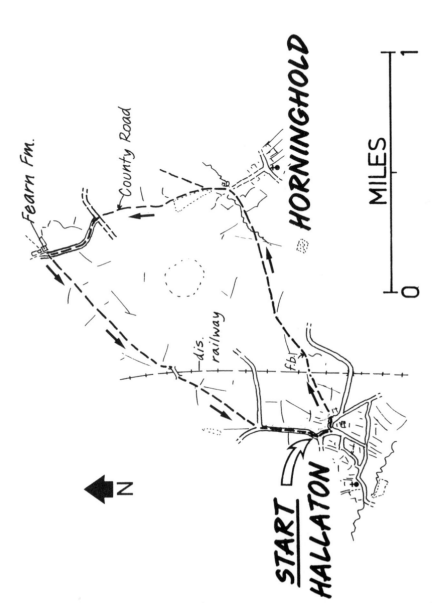

Good Leicestershire sheep country above Cranoe.

cross. The church (described by Pevsner as one of the most imposing in the county) stands at the far end of village. There is an excellent Norman tympanum, now in the porch, of St Michael and the dragon and much of interest inside and out.

Horninghold has an interesting church with a Norman doorway. Much of the village was created as a model village in the early part of the 20th century. (Note the initials of Thomas Hardcastle who was responsible for the new buildings.)
There are many large well-kept houses in beautiful grounds.

The walk From the Fox Inn by the duck pond in Hallaton take the Horninghold Road (North End) and after a few yards past a row of cottages turn left onto a path between modern houses and an older stable block. Go through black iron gates and over a stile. Continue downhill to the bottom left corner of the field. Cross the stile and go over the long-disused Melton Mowbray-Market Harborough railway line. Go straight over the opposite stile and footbridge into a huge field that is usually ploughed (The path should be cleared through standing crops.) Continue straight up through this field, over the brow of the hill and then down, aiming slightly to the left of Horninghold church spire. (The yellow waymarker post is towards the left hand end of a hedge of trees.)

Cross the wooden footbridge and go leftish across a narrow bit of field to cross another footbridge. Go through the next field on an ill-defined path, keeping a little away from the hedge on your left. Aim for a group of metal barns on the north end of the village. Go through a metal gate.

At this point, if you wish to explore the village of Horninghold you need to turn right, but to continue the walk we turn left.

To continue the walk from Horninghold go through the farmyard, past a metal gate and over a stile. Follow a stony track keeping close to the hedge on your left, aiming for a white house (Fearn Farm) on the skyline. Go through a metal gate and continue in the same direction to a double wooden gate onto the road.

Cross the road and walk up the farm road to Fearn Farm.

From Fearn Farm follow the Leicestershire Round signs at the wide gates of the sheep pens opposite the house. Keep close to the hedge on your right for two fields. Cross the double stile and continue in exactly the same direction across the huge ploughed field . (It might help to aim for the spinney near a railway bridge which is ahead at this point.) Cross the footbridge over the stream. Do not cross the railway bridge ahead but swing left, to reach the next (waymarked) bridge. Go over the old railway line and go down the slope. Keep in this direction, but cross the hedge on your right and continue close to it. Cross the stile in the corner of the field.

Make for the top right hand corner of the next huge field. There is a footbridge crossing halfway along the ditch in the dip. Meet the Hallaton road at the junction with Allexton Field Road. Follow the signposted road into Hallaton, passing the sports pavilion on your left.

The Fox Inn lies about a third of a mile along the road, by the duck pond.

From the Fox Inn you can wind your way down through the pretty village streets to reach Hallaton church.

Diana Davidson : "Tea half way round at Fearn Farm is my idea of a real treat!."

HALLATON
14
Cranoe   Hallaton

How to get there A6 south to Kibworth. Then turn left and follow signs to Hallaton.

Car parking Roadside only. There is some space near the school in Church Gate. Use discretion and consideration.

Public transport Ring Busline.

Map Pathfinder Map 916 (SP79) Wigston and Kibworth Beauchamp.

Route A mix of pasture and arable fields. Lots of hills, with compensatingly fine views from the high ground. Hallaton sits very prettily in a hollow to the east of its old castle site.

Mileage Just under 5 miles.

Refreshment The Fox Inn, the Bewicke Arms and a village shop in Hallaton. The Bewicke Arms has tea rooms and an elegant craft shop.

Items of interest Hallaton, the scene of the Easter Bottle Kicking ceremony, is a village full of interest. The church is lovely and the houses round the green as pretty as a picture. After your walk a visit to Hallaton museum is worth while. Open May/Oct. Saturdays and Sundays 2.30 – 5pm
The route passes the site of the very impressive 11th century motte and bailey castle.

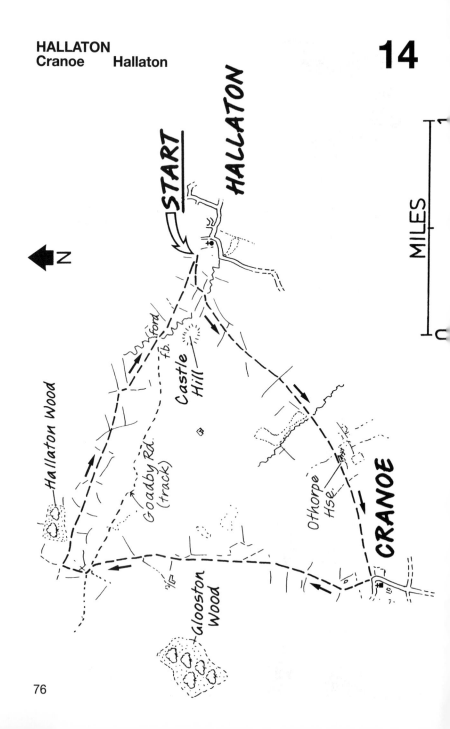

Langton Caudle Hill.

The walk *From Hallaton church walk up Churchgate. At the top, where the road bends right, go straight ahead through the kissing gate to the right of the little cemetery. Walk close to the hedge on your left and keep straight on, down the slope, to cross the stream. Turn left.*

Cross the wooden cartbridge and go up the hill moving slightly to your right. Keep parallel with the hedge on your left, but not too close to it. The crossing point is at the top of the field about 100 yards from this hedge.

Continue uphill, moving further away from the hedge on the left and cross the waymarked fence on the skyline. Continue over the brow of the hill keeping in exactly the same direction. Pass close to a pond on your left and go through the waymarked handgate.

Aim for Othorpe House at the top of the hill beyond the valley. Go downhill to cross the footbridge just to the left of a spinney and continue uphill to the farm.

Cross the track. (Othorpe House, to your left, is all that remains of the Deserted Medieval Village.) Go between the barns. Pass the redbrick barn on your left and turn left and right to pass metal sheds.

Cross the little paddock, close to the hedge on your right. Continue parallel with a hedge over to your right as you continue along the hillside. When the hedge begins to bend and go downhill, cross through the gap and keep straight on across the next, undulating, field, Aim for the top left corner and keep straight on past the isolated telegraph pole to reach the gate which leads onto the road opposite Cranoe church. Do not go through the gate but turn sharp right.

Here we leave the Leicestershire Round and follow the Midshires Way. Walk uphill, still in the same field, close to the hedge on your left. Continue to the top of the field. Go through the iron gate. Continue straight ahead keeping the hedge and small ditch on your left. On reaching the next iron gate look to your left and you will see Glooston Wood in the distance. Continue straight ahead (due north) towards the waymark on the far side of this long field.

Pass through the five-barred gate and continue ahead close to the hedge on your left. On reaching the farm track turn left through the gap in the hedge and then turn immediately right. From this point you have a wonderful vista of the surrounding countryside.

Keeping close to the hedge on your right, walk for about 250 paces then go over the stile on your right. Hallaton Wood is over to your left.

Keep in the same direction, bearing slightly right to go through a gap in

The ford below Langton Caudle hill.

the hedge and then carry on towards Hallaton church, which stands among trees some distance ahead.

Go down the slope to discover the stile well hidden in the hedgerow. Cross this stile and then bear slightly right through a small field to the next stile. Cross over a metalled farm track and continue down the hill, keeping Hallaton church spire dead ahead.

Cross the stile in the far corner of the field and scramble down the grassy bank to the metalled farm road. Turn left along the road and cross the ford (or use the footbridge to the right of the ford if the water is deep.) As you continue up the hill you will be passing Castle Hill over to your right.

At the bend in the road go straight ahead on the signposted footpath, through the five-barred gate and continue close to the hedge on your left. Go over the stile in the corner of the field and bear slightly right to reach the church, where the walk began.

Alec and Bernie Mansfield : "A very pleasant walk and not too strenuous. At various spots there are lovely views for you to enjoy."

GLOOSTON
Stonton Wyville   Glooston

15

How to get there Glooston village can be reached by turning left in Kibworth from the A6 going south from Leicester. Proceed through Tur Langton towards Hallaton. Fork left after about 2 miles.

Car parking Roadside only

Public transport Very sparse bus service. Ring Busline.

Map Pathfinder 916 (SP79) Wigston and Kibworth Beauchamp.

Route Undulating. Good views.

Mileage 3 and a half miles.

Refreshment Mill Farm, Stonton Wyville, on the road towards Tur Langton, now serves refreshments at weekends in the summer or by arrangement. The Old Barn at Glooston does not usually open for food during the day.

Items of interest The church in Glooston is much restored. Its graveyard is massed with aconites and snowdrops in early spring. Stonton Wyville is a small hamlet with its tiny 13th century church and interesting monuments to the Brudenall family. (The Brudenalls still

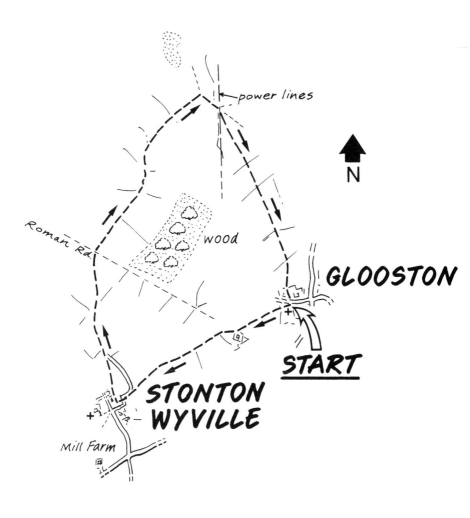

power lines

N

Roman Rd.

wood

GLOOSTON

START

STONTON
WYVILLE

Mill Farm

MILES

0   1

St Leonards, parish church, Thorpe Langton.

own land in this area.) The remains of extensive fishpond gardens lie beside the old Manor House.

The walk crosses the Roman (Gartree) Road from Leicester to Colchester, crossing the Welland near Medbourne.

There is a lovely view from the northernmost point, as you turn back to Glooston, of Nosely Hall (early 18th century).

The walk *Start by the village hall in Glooston, where there is some parking space, at the end of the village street near the Old Barn pub. Take the path between the small church (on your left) and the village hall. In the open field aim for the pylon in front of you. Cross the stile to the right of the small water treatment works in the far corner.*

In the next three fields the willow-lined stream winds its way over to your left. The path goes in a straight line to Stonton Wyville with waymarked crossing points slightly to the right of the field corners. Meet the track and continue along it towards Stonton Wyville.

Here we leave the Leicestershire Round by turning right at the farm buildings (But it is worth going a little further to explore Stonton Wyville village. Return to this point, if you do.) From the farm buildings follow the very well defined track leading north uphill towards Nosely. After about half a mile, cross the line of the Roman (Gartree) road, marked by a signpost, and continue in the same direction along a bridle path with the hedge on your right for five fields (a mile). Pass several signs to Nosely.

Turn right at a signpost marked Glooston/Goadby to reach a gate directly under a power line. Go through the gate and move slightly away from the power line, staying roughly at the same height, passing a large marker post in the middle of the field. Cross the double stile in the middle of the opposite hedge. Go straight on to the next stile, through another field, keeping close to the hedge on your right. Aim for Glooston village ahead. Near the village, aim for an unobtrusive stile to the left of a tall poplar tree and proceed through the farmyard to come out by the village hall, where the walk began.

Diana Davidson: "An easy short walk through typical east Leicestershire farmland."

STONTON WYVILLE 16
Thorpe Langton   East Langton   Church Langton

How to get there Stonton Wyville lies south east of Leicester, due north of Market Harborough. Turn off the A6 at Kibworth and go through Tur Langton. Follow signs towards Hallaton.

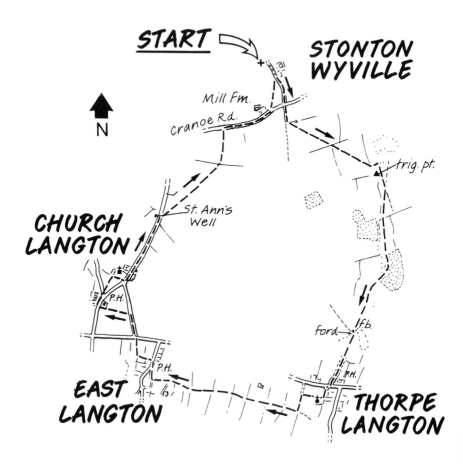

Car parking There is usually space on the field road at the start of the walk.

Public transport 144 bus from Fleckney goes through Thorpe Langton, very occasionally. You could start the walk from there. Ring Busline.

Map Pathfinder 916 (SP79) Wigston and Kibworth Beauchamp.

Route A climb up the Caudle then gently downhill and flattish. Beware mud in the narrow gateways at the foot of the hill and the ford in times of flood. Keep dogs under control. This is pasture country with very pretty villages. Views over the Welland valley towards the wooded hills of Northamptonshire.

After the climb up to the Caudle the walk goes through flattish pasture and arable land with wide views across the Welland valley.

Mileage 5 miles.

Refreshment The Mill House at Stonton Wyville serves coffees, afternoon teas, meals (at weekends and bank holidays) and provides accommodation.
Pubs at Thorpe Langton, East Langton and Church Langton.

Items of interest Stonton Wyville is a little village with a grand house and small church with Brudenell family connections.
A windmill once stood on the top of Langton Caudle. Views of all the Langton church steeples, Church Langton with its most impressive tall tower, Tur Langton's redbrick spire, Thorpe Langton spire and West Langton Hall.
East Langton cricket field, a place to loiter in the sunshine.
Church Langton, with its splendid church in golden greyish stone, is famous for its connections with the rector William Hanbury, whose bequests provided musical festivals, charity schools and woods. The school founded for the education and religious instruction of boys and girls of the parish by William Hanbury MA Rector of Church Langton in 1767 and erected in 1873 is now the Hanbury Centre.

The walk *From Stonton Wyville church walk back to the Kibworth-Cranoe road. Cross the road and follow the field road, signposted to Thorpe Langton, for a hundred yards.*
(It is possible to follow this track beside Langton Caudle all the way to the ford. As the ford may be impassable in wet weather, we suggest the prettier route over the top of Langton Caudle.)

Turn left at the bridleway sign (signposted to Welham) and go diagonally uphill to reach the top left corner of the field. From the gate walk uphill with the hedge on your right. At the next fence turn left (ignoring the handgate ahead) and walk along the contour of hill with the fence on your right. Cross the hedge and continue with it on your left. Ignore the handgate on your left and go through the one in the far corner of the field.

Turn right and walk with the hedge on your right to reach the trig point. Continue downhill from the trig point with the hedge on your right. Cross the stile at the foot of the hill and continue along the long sloping scrubby valley pasture to the spinney at the far end. Go through the spinney on a well trodden path and swing right to enter the next long pasture field. (Move slightly uphill to avoid the worst of the wetness by the spring.) Go down to the ford, by the bottom right corner of the field.

Cross the footbridge beside the ford and continue up the track to Thorpe Langton, emerging by the Bakers Arms (on your left), opposite the telephone kiosk. To reach Thorpe Langton church turn right, along the road and then left. Turn right to pass close to the church on your left.

From Thorpe Langton church follow the walled green path which leads into an open field and continue to the redbrick farm ahead (dated 1823 in brick patterning) Turn left here and follow the green lane into the open field ahead. Turn right to follow the hedge on your right.

Follow the series of waymarked stiles. Pass Park Farm uphill to your right. In open fields move very slightly right. Follow the hedge over to your left in two fields. As you approach the houses of East Langton, move slightly right of the field corner to cross the last little field. Go straight across this and then swing sharp left up a short length of old hedged way. Cross the fence and turn right along the road to East Langton to pass the Bell Inn on your right.

Turn left at the footpath sign and keep close to the left hedge of the cricket field. Follow the waymarks and turn right to reach the road at the T-junction with Church Causeway to Church Langton. You could continue on this road all the way to the church, but I prefer to turn left and take the footpath to the pub. Cross the signposted stile just past the house on your left and go straight across the field, following the line of ridge and furrow. In the next field you see the pub, with good views of West Langton Hall ahead. The footpath sign points you into the Langton Arms pub car park. Turn right at the road, passing the pub on your right. Church Langton green and the impressive red brick Georgian rectory lie ahead, in the fork of the roads. Go straight ahead and walk along a little path between redbrick walls of house and rectory. This takes you to the church. Turn right to go through the church yard.

Pass Church Langton church on your left and go down the road towards Stonton Wyville and Tur Langton. When the road begins to swing left and flatten out, turn right (opposite St Anne's Well) to go through a gate into the corner of the field. Go downhill, parallel with a fence over to your left. Cross the waymarked stile in the fence. Make straight for the Mill House with its distinctive mansard roof. Cross the stile into the corner of the field. Follow the straight hedge on your right to meet the road at the signpost.

Turn right along the road to reach Mill House and the Stonton Wyville crossroads. The church lies to your left.

Heather mac Dermid: "Give yourself time to wander through Church Langton and East Langton and to sample the pubs."

FOXTON
Gumley   Smeeton Hill   Foxton Locks   17

How to get there 14 miles south of Leicester, off the A6.

Car parking There is a playing field car park adjacent to the village hall and there is limited parking facing the church. Park considerately in side roads or use the Pay and Display car park at the picnic site on the Gumley Road.

Public transport A bus service operates between Market Harborough and Leicester but only via Foxton village on Sundays. Do check for times and changes by ringing Busline.

Map Pathfinder 916 (SP69/79) Wigston and Kibworth and 937 (SP68/78) Market Harborough.

Route A lovely mix of canal towpath then hilly pasture land. 1 mile canal towpath then gradually uphill to Gumley over pastureland, returning over similar terrain to the canal, then half mile back to Foxton along metalled track. The walk is pleasantly varied offering good views over the Leicestershire countryside.

Mileage 5 miles.

Refreshment Pubs at Foxton and Gumley and cafe at Foxton Locks.

Items of interest Foxton Locks, a unique staircase of ten locks. You can pause to see the boats going through the locks and visit the museum if you wish when you reach the canal wharf. Cross bridge number 62 to reach the staircase of locks on the far side of the wharf. If you have children with you do please pay attention to the warning sign

FOXTON
Gumley   Smeeton Hill   Foxton Locks

17

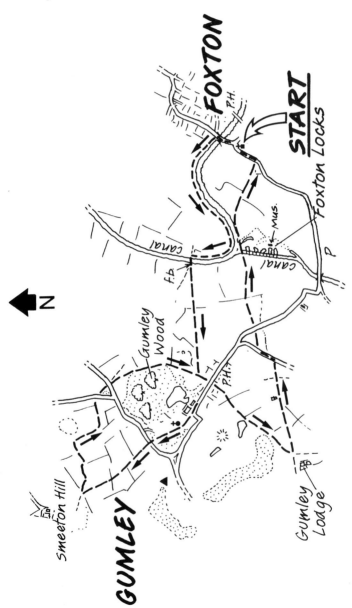

The staircase of ten locks at Foxton.

about deep water and strong currents. You will find toilet facilities here and refreshments are available at the shop, open 364 days a year, and the pub which is aptly named "Bridge 61". To visit the museum take the track to the right just beyond the pub. The museum is housed in the former boiler house of the Inclined Plane Boat Lift sited between the two flights of five locks.

The walk *From Foxton church walk the few yards down the road to cross the bridge over the canal. Turn left to join the Leicestershire Round footpath and walk for three quarters of a mile along the towpath, with the canal on your left, to the wharf at Foxton Locks and the junction with the Grand Union Canal.*

Keep the canal on your left until you reach Bridge 63, a high and narrow footbridge. Turn left to cross the bridge and continue in the same direction, away from the canal and west, towards Gumley. The church spire is in the wooded hill ahead, slightly to your right and the houses on the hill slightly to your left.

Pass to the left of a small sewage treatment works and cross the stile on your right. Go diagonally across the field to cross another stile. Turn left to follow the ash trees uphill and join a passageway which leads onto the Gumley village street. The Bell Inn lies to your left and the church to your right. Turn right towards the church.

At the first bend in the road go straight ahead towards Gumley church, through the kissing gate, then take the footpath at the left hand side of the church. Go through the kissing gate and make for the right hand corner of the field.

Cross the road to the footpath sign opposite and continue down the fields keeping close to the hedge on your right. There are splendid views from here with Saddington Reservoir visible ahead on your left, the village of Smeeton Westerby on your right, and the gorse scrub of Smeeton Hill ahead.

At the foot of Smeeton Hill you leave the Leicestershire Round. Cross the stile but do not go up Smeeton Hill. Turn right and follow the hedge for about 30 paces. Cross the stile on your right. (This will take you back towards Gumley but via a different route.)

Follow the hedge on the right as it zig zags round the field and cross the stile into the next field. Here there is a dip in the land. Keep close to the hedge and go over the double stile on your right. Keep in this direction to the end of the field. Cross the stiled footbridge. Turn left into a grassy tree lined track to reach the Gumley Road. Turn right and walk along the road to cross the road junction into the field and over to the left hand corner of Gumley Wood. Follow the edge of the wood closely until you come to a stile, which takes you into the field with the line of ash trees that led you into Gumley village.

Cross the field and once again follow the line of ash trees up to the village's main street. The route from Gumley continues straight ahead on the bridleway on the opposite side of the road. (The Bell pub lies to your left. You might like to stop here before continuing!)

From Gumley the signposted bridleway leads you between houses. Go through the bridlegate into the high open field. Keep close to the hedge on your right, following the blue waymarks. Go through bridle gates into a field which slopes steeply downhill. Go down the sunken holloway which takes you to the left hand corner of a small lake hidden in trees (The Mot). Bear slightly left over the next field keeping to the hedge on the right. Cross a farm track and head towards Gumley Lodge.

Turn left at the bridle gate, leaving Gumley Lodge on your right. Follow the hedge to meet the drive to Gumley Lodge. Do not follow the drive as it bends right but take the grassy path ahead. Cross the stream and keep close to the hedge on your left until you meet the road.

Turn left along the road for about 50 yards. At the bridleway sign turn right to cut off the corner to the next road. Cross this road. The Foxton Locks Museum stands on raised ground ahead and to the right. Follow the hedge on your left at first and then continue, bearing slightly right, through the long field and along a short track to the foot of the locks.

Cross over the canal by the bridge and continue straight ahead past the shop and the pub following the metalled track, back to the main road through Foxton. Turn left to return to the church.

Gillian Smith.

"Stop at the Foxton Locks wharf on your way back, to reflect on this very pleasant walk before you follow the metalled track and road back to Foxton church."

GUMLEY
Saddington   Saddington Reservoir   Gumley **18**

How to get there The walk could be started from either village. They lie south-east of Leicester, between the A50 and the A6. They can be reached via Fleckney or Kibworth and Smeeton Westerby.

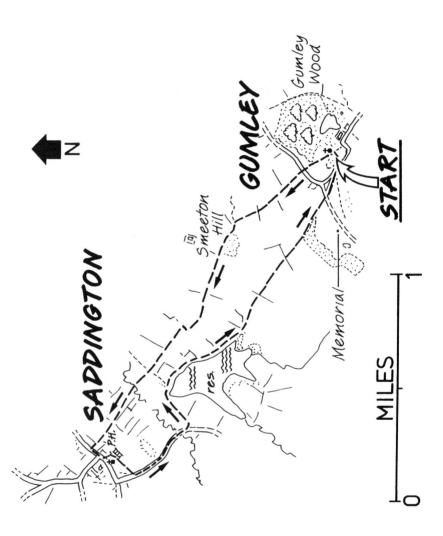

The war memorial cross near Gumley.

Fine willows alongside Saddington Reservoir.

Car parking On main village street only. Use care and consideration for others.

Public transport No regular bus service.

Map Pathfinder 937 (SP68) Market Harborough.

Route Quite steepish hills across lovely pasture land with beautiful views then a quiet reservoir lane.

Mileage 4 miles.

Refreshment The Queens Head pub in Saddington has excellent views from its garden over the reservoir valley. The church serves teas on Sunday afternoons in the summer.
The Bell at Gumley serves good food.

Items of interest Saddington reservoir, popular with anglers and water birds.
Gumley is built on a lovely site. There was a settlement here in Mercian times. The Mercian kings met at Gumley in 749 and 775 AD
The Church was rebuilt 1759.
Gumley Hall, built by Joseph Cradock in 1764, has now gone. Cradock was a friend of Dr Johnson and the actor Garrick. He spared no expense on the house and built a private theatre in it but ran into debt and was forced to sell it. He died modestly aged 84. Only the stable block remains, now converted into housing.
The woods are one of Hanbury's plantations. The Rev. William Hanbury (1725–1778), who became vicar of Church Langton in 1753 when he was 28, had already done gardens and plantations at Gumley and Tur Langton. He believed there could be large profits from scientific tree planting. At Gumley the plantation was for several years the local tourist attraction. The gales of 1756 "blasted the tops of my elms and ashes."

───────────────────────────────

The walk *From Gumley, pass close to the church on your right and go through the spinney. Cross the open field near two magnificent beeches to the far corner. Cross the road and walk close to the hedge on your right, downhill for three fields towards Smeeton Gorse hill and then uphill close to the fencing on your left.*

From the top of the hill you have fine views all round. Smeeton Hill farm lies over to your right. The path crosses the open corner of the field, near the gorse. Move slightly right to continue along the hill side, close to a hedge on your right.

When the hedge ends, keep in the same direction and cross into the corner of a huge ploughed field with a little brick barn in the middle of

Saddington Reservoir, built to feed the Grand Union Canal.

it. Follow the hedge on your left to the next waymarked stile, slightly to your right, and walk downhill close to the hedge on your right. Continue downhill to cross the footbridges over the streams (from Saddington reservoir on your left). Go straight uphill to Saddington village.

Cross the concrete cartbridge and move slightly left up the steep hill to reach the crossing by a big ash tree halfway along the little field ahead. Go up the middle of this small field and join the hedged path up the left side. This leads to Saddington village street opposite the old Baptist chapel.

At the Baptist chapel turn left through Saddington village, passing the Queens Head pub on your left. At the church turn left down a short lane, close to the church on your right. Go through Manor farm and continue on the farm track to meet the Mowsley Road.

Turn left and walk downhill on the road. Cross the stream and turn left onto the lane signposted to Gumley. This lane leads you past the reservoir on your right and eventually rises steeply uphill past Holloway spinney.

At the top of the hill pass a trig. point on your right. Gumley war memorial lies to your right, overlooking the village cricket field.

Continue straight ahead on the road into Gumley. (Lovely views to your right over hilly parkland.) The church lies in woods to your left. You can follow the little waymarked path which goes close to the church or continue on the road, to pass the old weighbridge on your right.

Geoff Martin. "The outward route is hilly, with lots of stiles. The Saddington reservoir return lane is very easy. Both are very pleasant.'

SADDINGTON
Shearsby   Arnesby   Fleckney   Saddington   **19**

How to get there Saddington is south east of Leicester. Turn off the A6 south at Kibworth and follow signs through Smeeton Westerby to Saddington.

Car parking There is no public car park. Use the roadside in a tidy and considerate way.

Public transport For details of bus services ring Busline.

Map Pathfinder 916 (SP69/79) Wigston and Kibworth Beauchamp.

Route The Leicestershire Round from Saddington to Shearsby then through undulating pastoral countryside, skirting Fleckney.

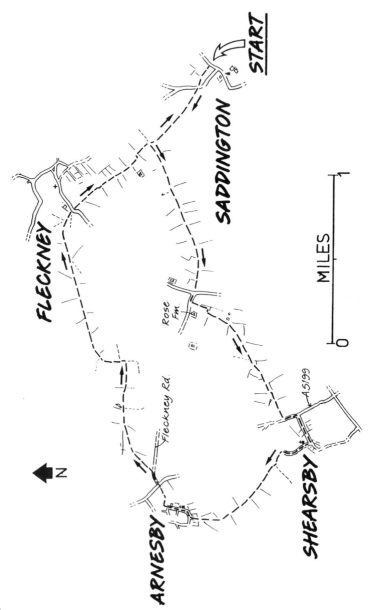

The Laughton Hills from near Saddington.

Mileage 5 and a half miles.

Refreshment The Queens Head Pub at Saddington, The Chandlers Arms at Shearsby, The Cock Inn at Arnesby all provide food and drink for thirsty walkers. The Dog and Gun at Fleckney is just off our route, at the end of Arnesby Road.
Tea and cakes are served in Saddington church on Sunday afternoons in summer.
Jacqui's tea shop is one mile from Saddington on the road to Mowsley.

Items of interest Saddington, views over the reservoir from the pub car park.
Shearsby thatched house a 17th century half timbered yeoman's house.
Arnesby Mill now a private dwelling.
Churches and interesting graveyards in the various villages.

The walk *From Saddington church walk along Main Street, passing the Queens Head pub on your right. At the road junction go straight ahead but turn left by the old Baptist chapel and follow the narrow walled lane. Continue through the farm yard, joining the farm track which swings left to meet the Saddington-Fleckney road. Cross into the field on the opposite side of the road. Walk with the hedge on your right. When you are about halfway along, turn right, over the three-stiled crossing and make for a large pond with bushes round it, in the middle of the big field.*

Pass the pond on your right and go through the gate ahead. (The village beyond is Fleckney.) Continue as if towards Fleckney Lodge for a few yards only, then turn sharp left, in the middle of the field, before the telegraph wires. Join the bridleway and keep close to the hedge on your right. Continue in this direction in the next field, with the hedge now on your left all the way to the road.

When you reach the road go straight ahead, towards Arnesby and Leicester, for about 200 yards. Turn left at the Leics Round sign before you reach Rose Farm. Follow the hedge on your left. Cross two stiles and then move diagonally right downhill over ridge and furrow. Cross the stile by a big stone horse trough.

Pass a hidden pond on your left and move slightly right, down the sloping field. Keep in the same direction in the next two fields, cutting across the field corners. Cross the cartbridge over the stream and turn right. Go gradually uphill to the top left corner of the field aiming for the big farm sheds.

Arnesby Mill and follies.

Continue close to the hedge on your left, and go through New Inn Farm yard (usually mucky underfoot) to meet the A50 Welford Road. (The house opposite was formerly the New Inn!) Turn left along the road and then turn right into Shearsby.

From Shearsby go to the end of Church Lane (passing the church on your right) and join the signposted footpath. Walk with the hedge on your left, cross the footbridge and turn right to follow the bank of the stream for a short distance. Cross a stile and turn left to head up over the brow of the hill. The stile is hidden in the far right corner of the field. The footpath is then well defined into Arnesby. It follows the hedge on the right and then goes through a short green lane and continues close to the hedge on the right.

Follow the road through Arnesby, passing the church on your right. When you reach an open green, turn right to follow the footpath which goes between the thatched house and a house named, rather curiously, 'Sea View'. Join the farm track to meet the A50 Welford Road. Cross with care and continue in the same direction along the road to Fleckney immediately opposite. After about 200 paces along this road turn left onto the footpath. Cross the first field diagonally. (The rounded cleft hill ahead on the distant horizon is Billesdon Coplow.)

At the end of the field turn right, keeping the hedge on your left. Pass to the right of an area of bushes surrounding a pit and go downhill to cross a small footbridge. The next stile is a short distance uphill. Cross it and go straight ahead. The next hedge is out of sight until you cross over the brow of the hill. Turn left when you reach the end of the field and walk with the hedge on your right until you meet a handgate. (Ignore the stile in the hedge.) Keep close to the hedge on your right as you go through the next field. The bridle route to Fleckney is now well defined. Follow it until you meet the Arnesby Road.

Cross Arnesby Road, Fleckney, and join the footpath a few yards to your right on the opposite side. This passes the rear of various properties. Pass a small recreation ground (suitable for a short break). Continue past Fleckney Lodge on your right. After a short distance meet a gate with a notice saying 'Private Road'. Cross the awkward fence just to the right of the gate. Continue in the same general direction but move very slightly left to rejoin the Leicestershire Round, keeping the hedge on your left for half a mile in a straight line back to Saddington, where the walk began.

Colin Hames.

Our foolproofer says: "I was surprised how pleasant this walk is. Leave time to explore the villages!"

SHEARSBY
Bruntingthorpe   Shearsby

20

How to get there Shearsby is nine miles south of Leicester, just off the A50/A5199.

Car parking Roadside parking with discretion at Shearsby. Lane between Arnesby and Bruntingthorpe, near bridge and sewage works.

Public transport Poor (United Counties X60). Ring Busline.

Map Pathfinder 916 (SP69) Wigston and Kibworth Beauchamp.

Route Easy walking. Well waymarked. Mud in places.

Mileage 3 and a half miles.

Refreshment Bruntingthorpe, The Plough (does not do meals) and The Joiners Arms (serves excellent food and drink).
Shearsby: The Chandlers Arms.

Items of interest The villages have a charming mix of houses. Shearsby has a thatched yeoman's house by the church. Pause to read the fascinating gravestone inscriptions (one to a priest who died in 1601 and one to William Weston, aged 36 who died in 1756 after the windmill sails caught him).
The nearby Bath Hotel is a reminder that there was once a salt spring here, and it was hoped that it could become a prosperous medicinal spa.
Bruntingthorpe is an old Anglo Saxon settlement which later acquired its Danelaw name. It was enlarged when it became an airfield in World War II and a US airbase.

The walk *From Shearsby crossroads, the church lies to your right, the village green lies straight ahead. (The Chandlers Arms lies to the left.) The road straight ahead goes round the village green and bends left along Back Lane to Mill Lane.*

From Mill Lane, signposted to Bruntingthorpe, turn right, into the field near the de-restriction sign. Walk close to the hedge beside the house on your right. Pass a pond on your left and continue with the hedge on your right. Continue through the tree-edged hollow, close to the fence on your right and keep close to the hedge on your right until you pass the tall poplar trees on your right. Cross the hedge, where it kinks and continue in the same direction close to it on your left as you go gradually downhill. Move slightly right to cross the footbridge at the bottom of the field.

Continue uphill, close to the fencing of a plantation of trees, and keep

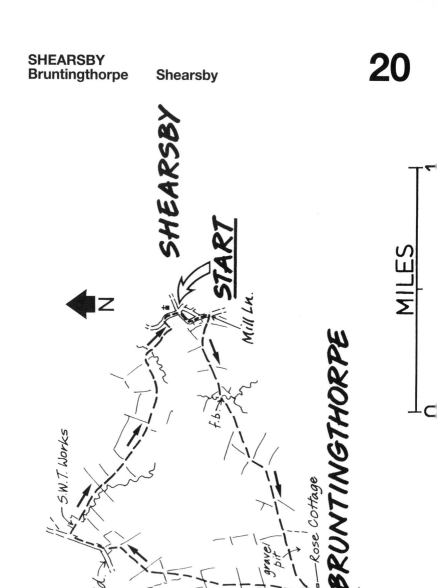

Yeoman's Cottage Shearsby.

in the same direction across a big (ploughed) field, aiming for a waymarked gate at the top of the hedge on your left. Cross the stile by the gate near the rising bank of the field and follow the hedge on your right. Pass a farm shed and follow the firm farm track in the next (very long) field. The track continues, curving slightly left to pass an old gravel pit on your left.

Here we are about to turn right, past an isolated ash tree, to leave The Leicestershire Round, but the pretty village of Bruntingthorpe with tempting pubs lies ahead. You could continue through the waymarked gate and walk along Little End to meet the main village street. The Plough is to your left and The Joiners Arms to your right, on Church Walk.

From Bruntingthorpe return to this point by going through the waymarked gate at the end of the lane near Rose Cottage and swinging left past an isolated ash tree.

The waymarked path now goes due north towards Arnesby. Keep in a straight line, crossing a series of waymarked stiles beside the gently meandering stream down to your left. (These fields are usually ploughed but reinstated by the many feet which walk the route.)

When the stream takes a bend and cuts across your path, swing slightly right and keep in this direction to cross waymarked stiles, aiming for the far right corner of a field beside a big ash tree. Continue diagonally right to cut off a corner of a little field. Cross the (parish boundary) hedge and look for a little brick building at the far side of the field and telegraph wires coming in from your left. Go straight across the field aiming for the telegraph pole to the left of this barn. The waymarked crossing is to the right of the telegraph pole. Cross the footplank (with care) and move left across the little field alcove, to meet the road.

Turn right and walk along the Lutterworth Road towards Arnesby for about 100 yards and then right onto a concrete road towards the sewage works. Continue along this road past the sewage works for approx 400 yards, then left onto a farm track through a gate. (There is a stile 10 yards to the left.) Keeping to the left of the field pass a barn and follow the hedgerow to your left to the corner of the field to a waymarked stile. Stay in line with the previous hedge, straight across the field to a marker post.

At the hedge turn left to a gate and then follow the contours of the field, bearing slightly left to a gate and stile on your left. Cross the field with the hedge on your right and cross the stile in the corner. Bear left to walk all the way round the field to the bottom corner, where you cross a stile and footbridge.

Keep the hedge on your right and walk uphill. Cross the stile in the corner and join a lane past cottages, new houses and Shearsby church.

Fred Heighton (Walked by Ted and Betty and Kate and Edward, who all enjoyed it.)

BRUNTINGTHORPE
Peatling Magna   Willoughby Waterleys   **21**

How to get there Bruntingthorpe is due south of Leicester. It can be reached via Countesthorpe or from the A50 (5199) via Arnesby and Shearsby.

Car parking No public car parks but there are some quite wide roads, for roadside parking. The road near Apple Tree House is a possibility . The road which comes from Shearsby has wide grass verges.

Public transport Virtually none! There may be a bus on a Wednesday!

Map Pathfinder 915 (SP49/59) Hinckley and Earl Shilton and 916 (SP69/79) Wigston and Kibworth Beauchamp and 936 (SP48/58) Lutterworth and 937 (SP68/78) Market Harborough.

Route Bruntingthorpe to Peatling Magna 2 miles, beside the stream. Peatling Magna to Willoughby Waterleys 1 and a half miles on headland paths in flat arable country. Willoughby to Peatling 2 miles through well waymarked pasture fields. Peatling to Bruntingthorpe 1 and a quarter miles over interesting little fields.

Mileage 6 or 7 miles.

Refreshment The General Elliott pub at Willoughby Waterleys does not serve food during the week.

The Shires pub, Peatling Parva and The Joiners Arms pub, Bruntingthorpe, both serve excellent food and drink. (B and B is available at The Manor House, Bruntingthorpe.)

Items of interest In Peatling Parva on the path which leads from opposite the church to the back of the hall you can see llamas in the field. All the villages have lovely buildings.

The walk *From Bruntingthorpe (where the little church is tucked away at the end of Church Walk) pass the garage and the Joiners Arms on your left and follow the main street towards Peatling Magna. Turn left at the footpath sign by the last house (Apple Tree). Cross the field moving to your right, away from the house. Cross the fence by an ash tree*

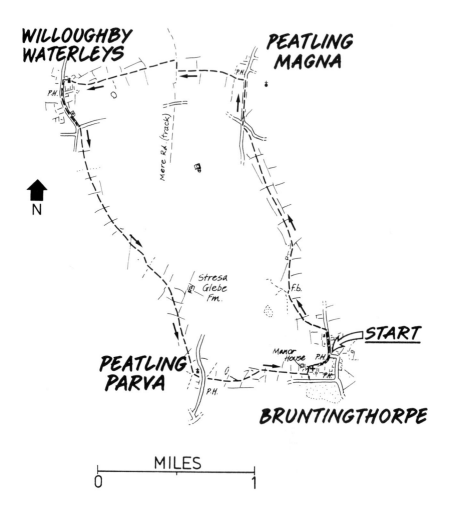

WILLOUGHBY
WATERLEYS

PEATLING
MAGNA

P.H.

Mere Rd (track)

N

PEATLING
PARVA

Stresa
Glebe
Fm.

f.b.

Manor
House

P.H.

P.H.

START

BRUNTINGTHORPE

P.H.

MILES

0   1

Spring in Aston Firs.

about 40 yards from the field corner. Continue in the same direction. Cross into the third field close to a hedge on your right.

Keep this hedge on your right but move gradually down to a (well-hidden) gate near the stream. Do not cross the footbridge on your left but keep straight on. You will be following this stream, keeping it on your left nearly all the way into Peatling Magna. Peatling church spire will come into sight, slightly right, ahead of you.

Move to the far left point of the last field, crossing the cartbridge to emerge at the crossroad junction. Follow the road uphill into Peatling Magna. The church lies in the field over to your right. (The Cock Inn lies ahead.)

Turn left at Postal Cottage, opposite the old Post Office (now called Hollow Tree Farm). The footpath goes along the drive between the house and the garage.

Follow the drive into the open field and cross to the right hand corner. Follow the hedge on your right for three fields, where you meet the old boundary hedged track (Mere Road).

Turn right for 100 yards along the Mere and at the gate turn left, into the field corner. Keep the hedge on your right all the way to Willoughby Waterleys going gradually downhill to cross the stream, and then up to the village. When the houses come into view you need to cross the stile in the hedge on your right (by the little cemetery). Follow the drive from the cemetery and swing right at the lane which leads round into the churchyard. Pass the church on your left.

From Willoughby Waterleys church turn left to walk through the village, passing The General Elliott pub on your right. At the first road junction (to Peatling Magna) turn left and then immediately right at the footpath sign. Keep close to the hedge, passing an old hall on your right. Continue through the gap in the hedge (double stile), bearing slightly diagonally left across a large field (sometimes divided temporarily into two).

Go over the next stile to the right of four ash trees. Continue straight across the next field, passing Willoughby Lodge farm on your right (a triple stile) and then follow waymarks for five further fields, eventually crossing Mere Road (now a mere track).

Continue to follow the waymarks, moving diagonally right for the next two fields, passing Stresa Glebe Farm over to your left. Then go diagonally left for 2 fields, passing a windpump on your right. Peatling Parva church tower appears ahead of you.

Pass the church on your left and meet the road. The Shires pub and the delightful village green of Peatling Parva are along the road to your right. The footpath sign to Bruntingthorpe is almost opposite the church.

From Peatling Parva church cross the road to the footpath almost opposite, signposted between fences, then take the right hand fork, to Bruntingthorpe. Cross the stream and go through an orchard of saplings, across another plank and up the steep bank. Bear left of the large tree ahead and take a moment to look back at the view of the village behind you.

Walk diagonally left for two fields and then diagonally right for one field. Turn right immediately alongside the hedge and fence. Pass through a small farmyard with the Manor House on your left and then turn right onto the driveway. At the junction with the road take the footpath on your left towards Bruntingthorpe church and continue through the churchyard. Follow the tarmac strip path and continue along the lane (Church Walk). Pass The Joiners Arms pub on your left.

Meet the main street of Bruntingthorpe, where the walk began.

Margaret Chandler.

Our foolproofer says: "A good number of stiles on this walk! This is typical south Leicestershire countryside. Easy to follow waymarks."

WILLOUGHBY WATERLEYS
Ashby Magna   Willoughby Waterleys   **22**

How to get there South of Leicester. Take the Countesthorpe road (Winchester Drive) from Blaby and continue south to Willoughby Waterleys

Car parking Roadside parking only in Willoughby Waterleys but the road is wide in places if you park discreetly.

Public transport Nil.

Map Pathfinder 915 (SP49/59) Hinckley and Earl Shilton.

Route Mainly flat. Very easy, with quite a lot of track.

Mileage 3 and a half miles.

Refreshment The Chequers Inn at Ashby Magna and The General Elliott at Willoughby do not serve meals at lunchtime but may allow you to consume your own food if you buy drinks.

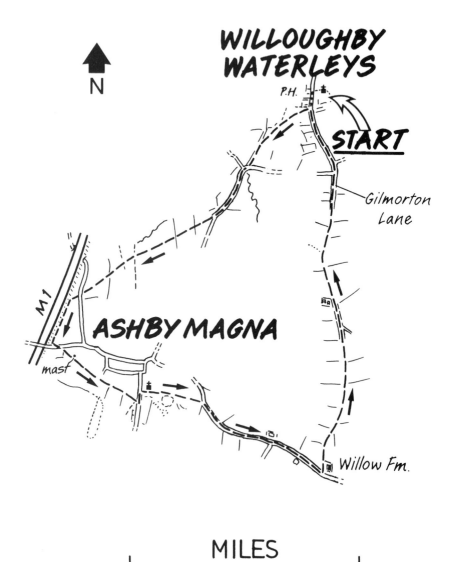

N

WILLOUGHBY
WATERLEYS

P.H.

START

Gilmorton
Lane

M1

ASHBY MAGNA

mast

Willow Fm.

MILES

0   1

Items of interest The moat near the church at Ashby.
The Old Hall at Willoughby.

The walk *From Willoughby Waterleys church cross the road and turn left to pass the General Elliot pub on your right. Pass Orchard Road and turn right at the footpath sign. Follow the tarmac strip into the open field and move slightly left to go up the slope, passing close to the telegraph pole. Go through the gateway, into the corner of the field with a hedge and stream over to your right. Move to the far right corner of this field and continue with the hedge and stream on your right until you reach the road.*

Turn right, pass the end of Cosby Lane and continue along the main Ashby-Willoughby road for about 300 yards. Turn right at the footpath sign and keep roughly parallel with the hedge over to your right. Keep in this direction across the next three fields to reach a gate and stile onto the green lane which leads into Ashby Magna, on your left.

Cross this green lane and follow the Leicestershire Round across the field to the M1 motorway. Turn left across the field beside the M1, go through the gate and up the steps. Turn left along the road for approximately 100 yards then cross the stile on your right. Cross two fields making for the waymark post at the right hand corner of a barn in the farmyard. Go straight over the third and fourth fields, heading for Ashby Magna church. In the next field go up the incline, slightly right to reach the road. Turn left to the church but turn right at the footpath sign just before you reach the church fence.

Pass the church on your left, cross the stile, then turn left through a gate and right, to go down the field, keeping the hedge on your right. (Pass the old moat ponds in the bottom corner of the field, over to your right.) Go up the slope to cross the stile by a trough and continue in the same direction to the road.

Turn right and follow the road for approximately half a mile. At the bend sign turn left onto the track beside Willow Farm. Follow this track all the way back to Willoughby. Cross Ashby Road and continue in the same direction, going straight on to reach Willoughby church, where the walk began.

Gladys Hudson. "This walk is suitable for winter as there is quite a lot of track."

LEIRE
Frolesworth   Leire

23

How to get there South west of Leicester. Can be reached from the A426 Lutterworth road. Turn off at Dunton Bassett.

Car parking Roadside only.

Public transport There are very infrequent buses. Ring Busline.

Map Pathfinder 936 (SP48/58) and 915 (SP49/59) Hinckley and Earl Shilton.

Route Gently up and down. Easy walking with good views.

Mileage 4 miles.

Refreshment Queens Arms and White Horse pubs at Leire.
The Plough and Harrow at Frolesworth.

Items of interest Frolesworth almshouses, founded in 1725 with ten later ones added in 1760 by Baron John Smith, a high flying local boy who remembered his birth place village in a generous and practical way.
The church has very interesting monuments and some 15th century glass.

────────────────────────

The walk *From Leire church walk down the road past the Queens Arms pub on your left.*

Turn left into Back Lane. Pass Wales Orchard on your left and continue on the metalled track, keeping in the same direction. (Ignore the right turn. Pass Hoke Court and houses on your left.) Keep on along the green lane and go straight ahead, over the neck of the field (the old disused railway track) and straight up the next field over the brow. Cross the double stile in the top corner of the field and continue in the same direction.

Cross the next stile in the corner of the field, beside a telegraph pole. Move gradually left towards Hillcrest Farm on the hill. Turn right and walk along the road towards Frolesworth for a mile.

Go straight over the crossroads, passing the old almshouses on the corner and the Plough and Harrow pub on your right, to reach Frolesworth church.

Pass Frolesworth church on your left and continue along the road towards Sharnford. Turn left opposite White Cottage. Follow a track between houses.

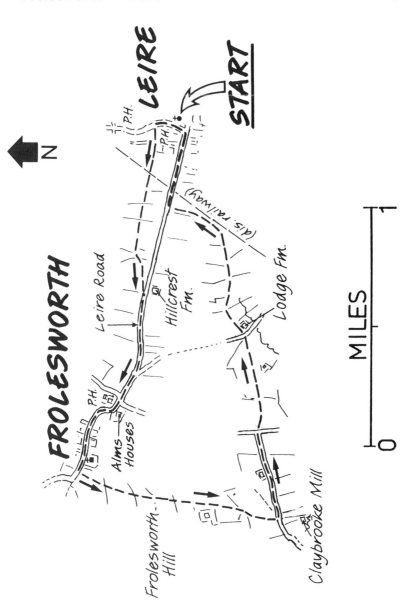

Continue in this direction (south) towards Claybrooke Mill. (In the first field walk close to the hedge on your left. Pass the rough remains of an old pond on your left and then continue slightly downhill, across the open field (usually ploughed) moving gradually away from the hedge on your left. Aim for Frolesworth Hill Farm, beside trees on the hill. Cross the waymarked footbridges and continue uphill to reach the farm drive, to the left of the farmhouse.

Pause to admire the views from this high point.

Continue downhill in the same direction, making for a cluster of trees in the dip of the valley. The footbridge is near the bottom right corner of the field. Cross the bridge and turn sharp right to walk to the corner of a small paddock. Pass close to the spinney on your left and continue with the hedge on your left until you reach the Frolesworth Lane (the road to Claybrooke Magna).

Turn left and walk along the Frolesworth road for half a mile. At the T-junction cross the road and continue in the same direction over the centre of the first field. Go through a gap in the projecting corner of the field and continue in the same direction through the centre of the second field to reach the house on the road ahead.

At the road cross to the footpath to the left of the house opposite. Cross the (very awkward) fence and walk close to the hedge on your right. Cross a second (very awkward) fence on your right. This takes you into the corner of a paddock. Go diagonally right to the next (awkward ladder stile) crossing.

Keep straight on in the next field, close to the hedge on your left. Continue up the hill to meet the line of disused railway. Go through the waymarked gap in the hedge and turn left to walk with it on your left and the railway line down below you on your right. Go through a gap on your left to emerge in the top corner of a field with a children's playground in the bottom right corner. Go down to this area, meet the road and turn right, to reach the church, where the walk began.

Mary Hodgkin.

Our foolproofer says: "Stop to admire the views across Leicester with the Charnwood Forest beyond. The walk gives you the chance to visit several interesting sites."

CLAYBROOKE PARVA
High Cross   Fosse Way   Claybrooke Magna

24

How to get there Claybrooke is ten miles south west of Leicester. Take the Narborough Road to the A5 then turn south on B577 and follow signs to Claybrooke.

Car parking There is a small lay-bye near Claybrook school, but this requires care and consideration for school use. Tidy and considerate roadside parking elsewhere, please.

Public transport Minimal. Ring Busline for help.

Map Pathfinder 936 (SP48/58) Lutterworth and 915 (SP49/59) Hinckley and Earl Shilton.

Route From the beautifully proportioned 14th century church at Claybrook Parva our route takes us through gently undulating countryside for a tranquil walk in the footsteps of the Romans from High Cross for one and a half miles along the pleasant hedged green track of the old Fosse Way, then across pasture fields to return via Claybrook Magna. Flat and easy walking.

Mileage 3 and a half miles.

Refreshment The Pig in Muck pub at Claybrook Magna and The Woodcutters on Bell Street.

Items of interest High Cross, the centre of Roman England, is at the junction of two important Roman Roads, the Fosse Way and Watling Street (now the busy A5). Our route takes the quiet Fosse Way. The High Cross monument, erected in 1712, is near the information board at the entrance to the Fosse Way.
Claybrooke Parva has a beautiful church (c.1340) in a lovely setting.

The walk *From Claybrooke Parva pass the church on your left. Follow the road towards Claybrooke Magna to reach the school. (Ignore the road to Monks Kirby and Brinklow on your left.)*

The route now passes to the left of the school grounds to reach the field behind it. At the footpath sign enter the field. Turn immediately right to pass the school. Go through a wide hedge gap and continue in the same direction. (NB The headland here is practically non-existent.) Keep the hedge on your left.

Pass a barn on your left and then move slightly right in a big open field where the hedge bends away from you. Go downhill to cross the footbridge and then walk uphill, slightly away from the hedge over to your left.

N

Claybrook Lodge Fm.

CLAYBROOKE MAGNA

Fosse Way

A5

High Cross Grange

High Cross

A5

Watling Street (A5)

f.b.

P.H.

CLAYBROOKE PARVA

Sch.

START

MILES

0   1

Burbage Common.

Make for the conifer trees of High Cross Grange on the hill ahead. Pass a protruding field corner on your right. The Grange is now in front of you. Go diagonally left into a narrow sharp corner of the field. Turn left at the road and walk to High Cross.

From the information board at the start of the Fosse Way follow the red Leicestershire Round waymarks along the green track for about 1 and a half miles. When the surface changes to a metalled surface, look out for Claybrooke Lodge farm over to your right.

Turn right, into the drive to Claybrooke Lodge Farm for about 20 yards and then go diagonally right, across the field. (The waymarks on this part of the route were missing when we last walked it.) Go through the gap in the hedge. Continue with the next hedge on your right. At the end of the field turn left for 10 yards then right to cross the stile and footbridge. Continue close to the hedge on your right and cross the stile and footbridge ahead.

Bear slightly left uphill, heading for a large tree slightly to the left of Manor Farm buildings. Cross two stiles into a hedged path leading into Manor Road, Claybrooke Magna, by the Pig in the Muck pub.

Cross the road and go through the gap by the footpath sign in the very tall hedge 10 yards to your right. Go up the stone steps to cross the stile and go diagonally down the field to cross the stile and footbridge in the far right hand corner.

Walk straight across the narrow strip of meadow and over the footbridge and stream into the grounds of the timber merchants. Walk carefully, close to the hedge and fence on your right.

Leave the timber yard over the (very awkward) stile and footbridge and turn left to follow the yard boundary. At the end of the yard boundary negotiate three stiles and enter the village of Claybrooke Magna. Cross the road bearing slightly right into Bell Street. (The Woodcutter pub is on your left.)

Towards the end of Bell Street, turn right at the footpath sign by house number 16. Follow the path to Claybrooke Parva, well used by local churchgoers. Keep the hedge on your left and follow the well kept route (part of the Leicestershire Round) over two fields, passing Claybrooke Hall in its beautiful parkland over to your left.

Meet the road opposite Claybrooke rectory. The beautiful church of Claybrooke Parva, where the walk began, lies to your left.

Chris and Jack Ingham.

How to get there Sharnford is south of Leicester, 2 miles from the Warwickshire border.

Car parking Sharnford has a public car park near the toilets on the main road.
Smithy Lane car park near Burbage Wood, off the Burbage-Sapcote Road near the M69, makes a good alternative starting point. Grid Ref. 452 945.

Public transport Sharnford and Sapcote are both on bus routes. Ring Busline for details.

Map Pathfinder 915 (SP49/59) Hinckley and Earl Shilton.

Route Easy walking in rather flat, mixed pasture and arable land, with some beautiful open areas and lovely woodland tracks.

Mileage 7 or 8 miles.

Refreshment May's Cafe, Wood House Farm near Burbage Wood, gives a good welcome to walkers. Sharnford and Sapcote both have welcoming pubs.

Items of interest Burbage Wood and the Common are well worth exploring. There is an information centre at Lynden Lea. (Grid Ref. 447 953)
On Sapcote recreation ground slight humps in the grass indicate the remains of a Norman castle mound (Toot Hill).
Aston Flamville has a dovecote dated 1715, in brick patterning.

The walk *From Sharnford pass The Countryman pub over to your left and continue straight ahead (on the right of the One Way triangle). Turn right along Aston Lane, passing Ivy House. Turn left keeping the old redbrick farm buildings on your left. Go through the small paddock, close to the fencing on your right.*

Keep in the same direction to cross the cartbridge and go through the gap. Pass the big modern grey farm sheds over to your right and continue in the same direction, close to the hedge on your right. Cross the stile (into a very muddy patch) and turn left to follow the same hedge. (Keep in the same direction to cross the open corner of the field.)

In the third field, with the tall spire of Burbage church ahead of you, walk close to the hedge on your right. When it bends, cross into the corner of a field and walk down to the footbridge over the stream Cross

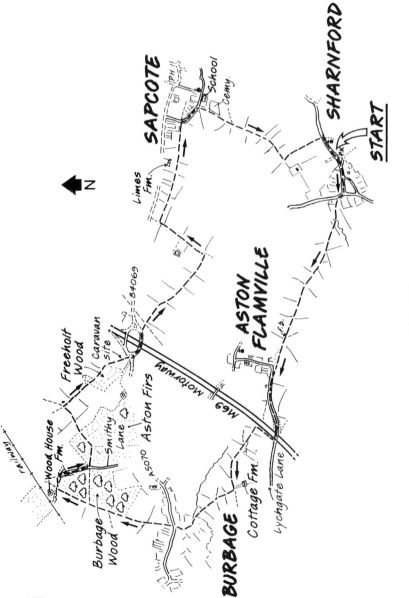

Burbage Wood.

the stile on the left. Cross the farm track and turn right to walk close to it.

As you go slightly uphill, the pretty hamlet of Aston Flamville lies to your right, just off our route. Join the lane on your right, and continue on the road towards Burbage, (Lychgate Lane). Cross the motorway bridge and turn right along the signposted farmtrack. Walk close to the motorway on your right and then turn left to reach a big pylon in the next field. Cross the stiles and footbridge in the field corner and pass the pylon on your right. Walk with the hedge on your left.

Burbage church spire lies ahead. When you see Cottage Farm, the redbrick house at the end of the next field, move right. Cross into the field on your right and walk close to the hedge on your left until you are level with Cottage Farm. Cross the stile. Our route to Burbage Common avoids Burbage. Turn sharp right, and with your back to Cottage Farm, walk towards Burbage woods, with Burbage church spire over to your left. Walk close to the hedge on your right, cross the stile in the corner and continue in the same direction across the open fields to reach the housing estate. Waymarked stiles lead into Sherborne Road. Follow this estate road round to the left to join Salisbury road and then turn right, into Winchester Drive.

Cross the main Hinckley-Sapcote road (A5070) and go through a gap between bungalows (nos 97 and 99) along a gravel path to a waymarked stile beside a gate, and into a field with a hedge on your left. Half way along this very long field go through the sparse hawthorn hedge and turn left to cross the stile. Continue in the same direction, but with the hedge now on your right.

Go through three large fields, passing Burbage Wood on your right. (Note that there is a good metalled track inside the wood, parallel with this footpath. You may prefer to use it.) Cross a plank cartbridge into the open field at the end of the wood.

(Wood House Farm, ahead to your left, serves teas to thirsty walkers.)

At the end of the wood turn right, to keep the woods on your right for about 100 yards. Turn right to go through a gate or gap into Smithy Lane Car park under the trees. Walk along Smithy Lane, passing one open field on your left (with more car parking) to the crossroads of tracks in the wood.

Turn left through the gate into Aston Firs Wood along a good stony path. At the end of the wood keep straight on, close to the hedge on your right, through two arable fields. (Grand views of Earl Shilton and Barwell over to your right.)

When you reach the third field turn sharp right. Keep the hedge on your right. Pass a small pond on your left. Go through two arable fields, which may be muddy, keeping close to the hedge on your right. At the end of the second field cross the stile into a lovely old meadow. Go straight across this meadow and cross the stile opposite, into Freeholt Wood.

Freeholt Wood is old and well coppiced. Go through this delightful woodland, keeping to the waymarked path. Emerge in a lovely meadow. Cross diagonally to the far corner, past a caravan site over to your right. Cross the stile and turn right to another stile onto a lane. Turn right to pass the caravan site entrance. Climb the iron railings on the left to the road by the M69 roundabout.

Cross the road and go anti-clockwise to the far side of the M69 roundabout, walking along the grass verge towards Sapcote. Go through a bridle gate on your right. Turn right. (The bridleway may be muddy in wet weather.)

At the corner of the field turn left, keeping close to the hedge on your right. Go under the power lines and continue on the bridleway through four gates. (Lovely views of Charnwood over to your left.) At the fourth gate turn left onto a green track for about 200 yards then continue straight on along a concrete drive. Just before you reach the busy Sapcote-Hinckley Road turn right at the footpath sign and cross the stile.

Keep the hedge on your right for four fields. Pass the Limes farm over to your left. In the fourth field cross the (slightly hidden) waymarked stile in the right hand corner of the field. Then go slightly left across the next field, keeping Sapcote church over to your right. Cross the next stile onto a narrow path between a fence and a hedge. Go about 100 yards to meet the road.

Cross the road and go onto a playing field by houses on your right. In about 200 yards, turn right at the footpath sign and go down a narrow path by the old rectory to reach the road, with the Sapcote primary school in front of you.

Turn right along the road and then left at the T-junction to follow a country lane (known to the locals as Donkey Lane). Pass the cemetery on your left and continue through a gate into pasture land. Pass through the next gate and follow a green track (which may be muddy in wet weather). After about 200 yards enter an open field, with a hedge on your right. Bear right and keep the hedge on your right to go through the bridlegate in the field corner. Turn sharp left and join a track, with Sharnford church in view.

The Coventry – Ashby de la Zouch Canal at Sutton Cheney.

Go through another gate, where the track becomes Mill Lane. At the bottom of Mill Lane turn right into Chapel Lane and left at the bottom to the main road. Turn right along the main road to reach your starting point in Sharnford.

Jean Farmer: "A very pretty walk although it involves crossing the M69 and skirting the urban areas of Hinckley and Barwell."

SUTTON CHENEY
Sutton Wharf   Bosworth Battlefield   **26**

How to get there Sutton Cheney is west of Leicester near Market Bosworth. Take the A47, B582 and B585.

Car parking Choose considerately a tidy roadside space. There are Pay and Display carparks at the battlefield centre and Sutton Wharf. You could start the walk from them.

Public transport Occasional buses. (Some routes run on a Thursday, some on a Wednesday, another Infrequently mid-week.) Ring Busline for details.

Map Pathfinder 894 (SK40/50) Leicester (West) and 915 (SP49/59) Hinckley and Earl Shilton.

Route Nice wide views in gently undulating countryside, looking over to Earl Shilton, Barwell and Stapleford church spires.

Mileage 5 miles.

Refreshment Two pubs in Sutton Cheney, Tea rooms at Sutton Cheney Wharf and at the battlefield centre and at Sutton Cheney Almshouses. A gourmet's delight!

Items of interest Sutton Cheney: The church of St James has memorials to Richard III, who prayed here before the battle in August 1485. The Almshouses were founded in 1612. Hall Farm dates from 1601.
Near Bosworth Battlefield site we follow part of the route of the Ambion Way (described in leaflets available from the battlefield information centre).
The Battlefield centre is worth a stop, for its shop, museum, tea place and toilets. If you have time and energy, you could add on a walk around the battlefield site, following the information boards beginning from the top of Ambion Hill and descending to Shenton Station (to see the steam trains and the field where Richard III was reputedly killed) and returning on a lower route, beside the railway line and swinging left

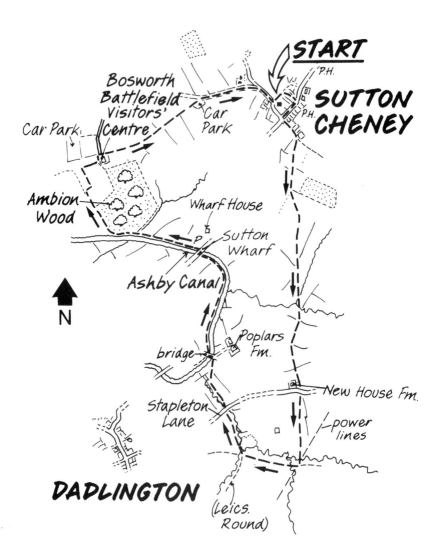

through woods on a well made gravel track, to reach King Dick's Well. You could however leave this extension for another occasion. It makes a lovely day out.

The walk From Sutton Cheney pass the church on your right and The Hercules pub on the left. At the road junction, turn left along the lane marked No Through Road. Pass Keepers Cottage on the right and continue to the big house on the left. Turn right through the field gap by the footpath sign. You now need to go diagonally across a series of three big fields, usually ploughed. If the path is left clear of crops, as the law requires, there is no problem. The first field is long and narrow with a wood over to the left and a long ditch down the middle. If it is obstructed by crops you need to make your way gradually away from the hedge on your right towards the right of the wood, to meet the ditch where it meets a hedge by a big gap in the field corner. Cross the waymarked plank bridge. In the second field you continue in the same direction to a gap in the far corner. Ignore the headland track which keeps close to the hedge. The third field is bisected by a long ditch. Aim for the far corner of the field, crossing the plank bridge over the ditch, by two hawthorn bushes. Continue to the end of the field and cross the waymarked footbridge into a smaller field.

Move slightly left in this pasture field and cross the waymarked stile into the corner of the next field. Keep parallel with the hedge on your left going gently uphill for one field and then bear left towards the left side of the farm ahead (New House Farm).

Pass a telegraph pole on your left and the farm on your right. Cross the stile in the far corner of the field. Meet Stapleton Lane and turn left and then immediately right, on a waymarked farm track close to hedge on the left. The footpath actually moves slightly away from the track, towards a tall pylon, to a waymarked crossing where there is no bridge over the stream. You may find it easier to go down the farm track to cross the concrete farm bridge and then turn right, to walk with the stream on your right and the pylon on your left.

At the end of the field look for a footbridge on your left, near a huge willow tree and go straight across the next field, parallel with the hedge over to your right. The next stile is in the right hand corner of the field, near the wood.

Here we join the Leicestershire Round. Ignore the waymark which points to your left and follow the stream on your right. Meet a brick bridge on the Stapleford Lane and turn right for a short distance, then left into the corner of a field close to a hedge on your right.

This path is now waymarked with the Ambion Way logo of the crown in the tree, as we are approaching the Battlefield of Bosworth field (where Richard III lost his crown). You can usually see the flag flying on Ambion Hill, where the battle was fought.

Follow the hedge on your right until you are about 50 yards from the end of the field. Cross the stile on your right and continue, across the corner of the next field. Cross the stile and keep in the same direction across the next field to reach the canal bridge. (The building over to your right is Poplars Farm.)

Turn left to cross the canal bridge, and turn immediately left to reach the towpath. Turn left again and go under bridge no 33 on the Ashby Canal. Walk along the towpath with the canal on your right, and go under the next bridge, at Sutton Wharf.

Climb the steps to your left and cross over the bridge. (The road leads to Wharf House for refreshments and to Sutton Cheney village, if you need a short cut back to the start of the walk.) Turn left into the Sutton Wharf car park, where there is an information board about the Bosworth battlefield.

From the carpark at Sutton Wharf follow the route shown on the information board to the Battlefield centre at Ambion Hill Farm. The route is well maintained and waymarked. It begins by following the canal on your left and then enters Ambion Wood by a series of stiles and handgates. A wide, grassy track leads through the trees, swings right and emerges in an open field with Ambion Hill Farm, the Battlefield Visitors Centre, immediately ahead.

From the Battlefield Visitors centre your route continues past the centre entrance on your right and then turns sharp right along a wide well marked grassy track, which goes straight beside a hedge on your left to a small car park ahead on the Sutton Cheney road.

From the high ground here you can see the spire of Market Bosworth church in the woooded area to your left, and the little capped tower of Sutton Cheney church in front of you, slightly to your right.

From the small car park on the Sutton Cheney-Battlefield road follow the road towards Sutton Cheney. Swing right at the junction with Sutton Lane and continue past the Almshouses tea rooms on your left. Turn left up a little slope by the next cottage, to go through the handgate which leads into Sutton Cheney churchyard, where the walk began.

Wm Nicholson: "This is the best walk in the book!"

SUTTON CHENEY
Market Bosworth   Sutton Cheney

How to get there From Leicester take the A47 then the B582/585. Follow signs from the A447.

Car parking Only roadside parking in Sutton Cheney. A big public car park in the arboretum park on the Cadeby lane as you enter Market Bosworth.
Toilets in Bosworth park near the rangers' hut.

Public transport There are buses to Market Bosworth. Ring Busline

Map Pathfinder 894 (SK40/50) Leicester (West).

Route Level open country with woods and lakes.

Mileage 3 and a half miles.

Refreshment Pubs and tea rooms at both villages.

Items of interest Sutton Cheney church, the almshouses, the flowers in the gardens are delightful.
Market Bosworth would make a good stopping point as it has shops, pubs, tea rooms, toilets, a market and a reasonable bus service. It usually provides a marvellous display of flowers in the Leicestershire in Bloom competition.

The walk *From Sutton Cheney pass the church on your left and the Hercules pub on your right. Walk along the road to reach the Royal Arms pub. Turn left and go through the car park. Continue straight ahead across the (usually ploughed) field. Go through the gap and turn sharp right. Walk with the hedge on your right to the end of the field and go through the gap. (The track goes left down and round the edge of the field.) Follow the footpath diagonally across the field corner, aiming for the house ahead in Spring Wood. Keep close to the hedge on your left to reach the bridge over the stream. Go through a narrow 'neck' between the Duckery and Spring Wood*

Now walk uphill with Spring Wood on your right, to the isolated mock-Tudor farmhouse at the edge of the wood. Cross the lane and continue straight ahead through the clearing in the woods to join the avenue of trees which leads to Bosworth Park (1 mile) past Looking Glass pond and Oak Ring wood on your left. Go through the handgate at the end of the avenue into Market Bosworth Park and arboretum, near the Giant Hogweed enclosure. (Do not touch the hogweed!)

Aim for the gravel path ahead which leads you past the lake which is beyond the bank on your right and then beside the edge of the park on

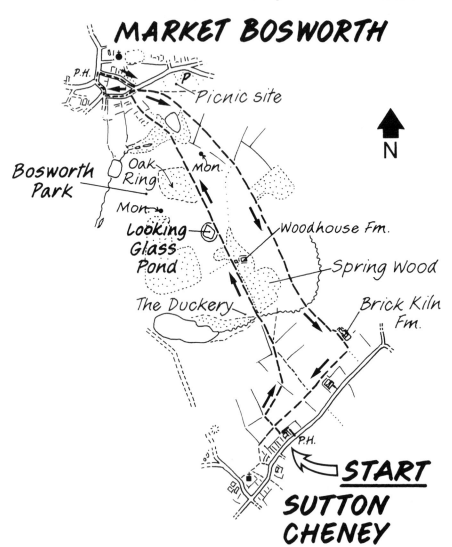

MARKET BOSWORTH

P.H.

P

Picnic site

N

Bosworth
Park

Oak
Ring

Mon.

Mon.

Looking
Glass
Pond

Woodhouse Fm.

Spring Wood

The Duckery

Brick Kiln
Fm.

P.H.

START
SUTTON
CHENEY

MILES

0   1

your left, aiming straight for Bosworth Hall and stables. (The car park can be seen diagonally over to your right.)

At the road turn left and then take the left fork to do a tour of the pretty village of Market Bosworth. (Rectory Lane and Sutton Lane lead you to the market square. The church lies to your right.)

From the market square of Market Bosworth turn right down Main Street, past the Dixie Arms and turn right again in front of The Red Lion to return to Bosworth Park to continue the walk.

Cross the park to reach the car park at the Cadeby Lane junction, passing it on your left. Take a direction between the lake on your right and the children's play area on your left. Cross the stile in the fence ahead of you. Cross the pasture field and the stile in the fence ahead. This takes you into the corner of a field. Walk close to the hedge on your left. (There are fine views of Cadeby through a gap in the hedge.) Pass the edge of a wooded patch (The Gorse) Continue with the hedge on your left. At the end of the field cross another stile, ignoring the right fork in the path. Walk straight on, slightly downhill, to the corner of the field. Cross the stile and footbridge (NB no dogs allowed here). Cross the field going diagonally left to the yellow marker post at the entrance to the farmyard of Brick Kiln Farm.

Pass through the farmyard and cross the stile in the right hand hedge Make for the large house with conifer hedging. At the brow of the field you should see the marker post in the dip ahead and a choice of two further yellow markers ahead. Choose the right hand marker and retrace your steps back to the car park at the back of the Royal Arms public house.

Turn right along the road to reach Sutton Cheney church, where the walk began.

Grace Allen: "Delightful in all seasons, with blackthorn and woodland flowers in March and bluebells and chestnut blossom in May."

MARKET BOSWORTH
Carlton   Market Bosworth

28

How to get there From Leicester take the A47 Hinckley road. Turn off on the B582/585 to the A447 then follow the signs to Market Bosworth

Car parking Market Bosworth has several small public car parks (but note that Tuesday is market day!) There is a big car park in the arboretum park at the junction of the B585 and Cadeby Lane.

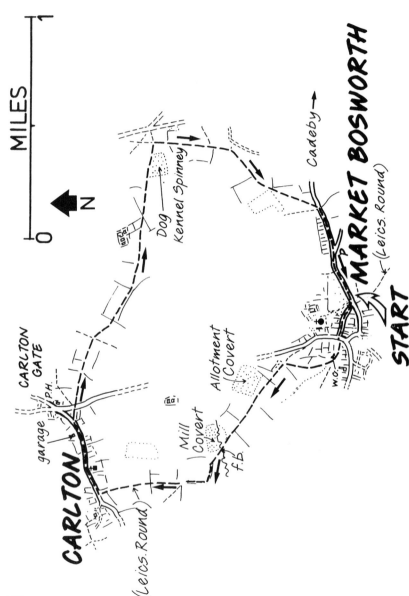

MILES

N

Cadeby →

MARKET BOSWORTH

(Leics. Round)

START

Dog Kennel Spinney

P.H.

CARLTON GATE

Allotment Covert

garage

P.H.

W.O.

Mill Covert

f.b.

CARLTON

(Leics. Round)

Public transport There is a bus service to Market Bosworth. Check with Busline.

Map Pathfinder 893 (SK20/30) Tamworth and 894 (40/50) Leicester (West).

Route The outward section (on the Leicestershire Round) takes you across beautiful countryside, in slightly hilly arable land with superb views from the high ground. The return to Market Bosworth is quite a difficult walk as there are many stiles and two potentially very wet and muddy areas. Also, beware of a couple of electric fences put by farmers across their fields.

Mileage 5 miles.

Refreshment Market Bosworth has a variety of pubs, shops and cafes. At Carlton the pub is on the main road at the far end of the village.

Items of interest Market Bosworth's market charter dates back to 1285 and from the central market square the town has expanded fanwise.
Bosworth Arboretum park with its well laid out woods, gardens, ponds, playing and picnic areas is ideal for family outings.

The walk *From Market Bosworth market place cross Main Street and continue in the same direction down Back Lane. Pass to the right of the old Dixie grammar school and the impressive old bank.*
Pass the public toilets on your right and continue downhill. At the T-junction cross the lane and enter the corner of the field just slightly to your left. There are two paths in this field. Take the one on the right. Walk downhill on a grassy track, close to the garden fence on your right. Cross the stream and make your way to the far right corner of the field, swinging gradually right to skirt a grassy mound on your right. The church spire is visible over to your right.

Meet the farm lane and turn left, past the houses. The lane becomes a farmtrack and then continues in the same direction as a field headland. Keep close to the hedge on your left. Pass Allotment Covert over to your right. At the end of the next very long field, Mill Covert comes in from your right to join a spinney plantation in the pointed corner of the field. Keep in the same direction to go through the spinney, keeping close to the stream on your left.

Cross the footbridge over the stream. Carlton church tower lies straight ahead but the footpath goes left to cross the hedge on the left of the field, near a telegraph pole. Walk around the corner of the field on your left. In approximately 100 yards go left over a stile and turn right. Walk towards Carlton close to the hedge on your right in the next three fields. Meet the road and turn right.

Carlton village with its quaint bell tower is to your right.

From Carlton walk along the village street, passing the church on your right and then a garage on your left. At the junction turn right, away from the public house on your left. Shortly, in the hedge on your left, note the two waymarked routes. Take the second arrow on the gate/stile into the field, with the farm on your right.

Continue straight ahead to the stile on the left of the gate, keeping the hedge on your left. (Note the view of Bosworth church to your right and Nailstone to your left.) At the bottom of the field cross over the double stile and the (dried-up) stream, keeping close to the hedge on your left. Next comes a very difficult stile in the hedge, which leads into what may be a very wet, muddy area.

From this marshy area proceed diagonally right to cross the stile and footbridge over the stream. Cross straight over the meadow to another gate and stile in the hedge.

Walk along the ridge, pausing to look at the view before continuing with the hedge on your left to the end of the ridge. Swing right across the field to an electricity post with a waymark arrow and proceed in this direction to go over a stile by a gate. In about twenty yards turn into an arable field. (The path may not be cleared here.) Aim for the corner of Dog Kennel Spinney and walk with the spinney on your right. At the end of the wood, turn right to cross the stile into a pasture field and swing diagonally right to cross two footbridges with stiles.

Cross the arable field (usually reinstated) bearing right to reach a gap in a clump of holly bushes in the hedge. Turn right and keep the fence on your right and cross the stile in the corner of the field. Continue over the fence near the hedge and continue straight on close to the hedge on the right. Turn left to follow the direction of the waymark arrow on the post. Cross over very marshy ground to a stile and footbridge at the corner of Cowpasture spinney. Continue diagonally up the field towards houses on the Market Bosworth road. Go over the cattle grid onto the road by the gate house and turn right. Pass Market Bosworth hall on your right and the parkland on your left. Continue along the road, taking the left fork of the one-way system and turn right at Sutton Lane, to enter the market place, where the walk began.

Grace Allen: "A very nice walk! Market Bosworth often wins the Leicestershire in Bloom competition and its flower displays are a joy to behold."

Thornton Reservoir.

CARLTON
Shackerstone   Odstone   Barton in the Beans   **29**

How to get there Follow the A47 westwards towards Hinckley. Turn right on the B582 to Desford and Newbold Verdon and the B585 to Market Bosworth. Carlton is two miles north of Market Bosworth.

Car parking Street parking only in the village. Use discretion.

Public transport There is a bus service from St Margaret's Bus station to Carlton (currently Route 153). Ring Busline.

Map Pathfinder 893 (SK20/30) Tamworth.

Route Easy walking in gently undulating countryside. Pleasant villages en route.

Mileage 5 miles.

Refreshment Manor Farm, Barton in the Beans. Mrs Jackson makes home made teas.
Shackerstone pub and tea room at railway museum.

Items of interest Carlton village has a little church with a quaint bell tower and spme pretty village houses.
Shackerstone has a castle site mound. The canal has colourful boats. There is a railway museum and it is possible to take rides on the steam trains.

The walk *From Carlton pass the church on your left and walk along the road towards Congerstone. Pass the old school (now converted to a house) and turn right along Shackerstone Walk. Pass the green and cross the stile at the left of Glebe Farm and follow the green, walled track. When it ends turn sharp left to pass big barns on your right. Keep in the same direction until you reach the end of the field on your right. Turn right and walk close to the hedge on your left. (The big barns are in this field.)*

Cross the footbridge and walk uphill with the hedge still on your left. The stile in the top corner leads you into a hedged square. Keep in the same direction, with the hedge now on your right. Cross the footbridge. You now have a series of very wide, open fields, usually ploughed. Keep in a straight line through the waymarked gaps across the middle of these wide fields. In the fourth, smaller, square field cross the footbridge in the top left hand corner.

The next, huge, field is bordered by a long stretch of woodland. You need to reach the far right corner of this wood. Make for the isolated

CARLTON
Shackerstone   Odstone   Barton in the Beans   **29**

house, Keepers Cottage. Cross the road to the left of Keepers Cottage and continue in the same direction going diagonally left across the (ploughed) field, making for the right corner of Orange Hill Plantation, the wood which borders the railway line.

As you pass the corner of the wood you have below you a grand view over Shackerstone railway station, to the canal beyond, making a graceful curve around the old castle mound of Shackerstone.

Continue in the same direction. Cross the railway footbridge, passing the old station (now a museum and tea rooms) on your left. Stop to admire the Victorian railway and the canal. Turn right and follow the station approach track, beside the canal, down to the road junction. Move left to Turn Bridge and turn right to reach the canal towpath

(Shackerstone village centre, with church and pub, lies to your left.)

From Turn Bridge, walk with the canal on your left until you are opposite the old castle mound on the far side of the canal. Turn right and cross the field and go up the waymarked steps and over the railway line. Cross the footbridge over the stream and go straight ahead, under the bridge of the second railway line. Swing left to follow the hedge on your left and cross the stile 100 yards to the right of the corner of the field. Meet the field road and turn right. Continue on this (usually muddy) track for about three quarters of a mile to reach Odstone Hall.

From the top of the rise you have fine views.

Pass close to Odstone Hall on your left and then turn right at the footpath sign. With your back to the hall go downhill to the footbridge at the bottom of the field, passing to the left of a pond. The path from the bridge turns right and immediately left to follow a hedge on the left uphill for two fields.

At the top of the hill Barton in the Beans can be seen ahead. Nailstone church spire is to the left.

The next field has an enclosed path leading to a stile onto a track. Turn left on this track and meet the main road. Turn right to reach the cross-roads, near Manor Farm. Meet Main Street, Barton in the Beans, and turn right.

From Barton in the Beans pass the rather splendid Baptist chapel on your right. Ignore the first footpath sign through farm buildings on your left and take the next path, signposted to Carlton, through two lots of green iron gates a little further on. Turn left and pass the farm buildings. Cross the stile and go diagonally left across the field to a gate and continue to the far left corner of the next field.

The route is waymarked and Carlton church can be seen ahead. A stile and plank lead to a small field with a gap in the hedge opposite leading to a track. Turn right here and then after approx 40 paces turn left. Keep close to the hedge on your left in a long field. Two more well waymarked fields lead to a small rough field with a stile leading to an enclosed path and a stile onto Main Street, Carlton, opposite the church, where the walk began

Mary Hodgkin.

NAILSTONE
Bagworth   Barlestone   Nailstone

30

How to get there Leave Leicester on the A47 west towards Hinckley. Turn right along the B582 signposted to Desford and Newbold Verdon and Barlestone. Turn right after Barlestone and follow A447 to Nailstone.

Car parking Roadside only

Public transport Ring Busline.

Map Pathfinder 894 (SK40) Leicester (West)

Route This is former mining country, now part of the National Forest. The reclaimed spoil heaps are newly planted with trees. There are attractive views from the higher ground.

Mileage 5 miles

Refreshment Pub in Nailstone. Several pubs in Barlestone.

Items of interest Churches in Nailstone and Barlestone. In Nailstone church there is a monument to Thomas Corbett, a gentleman who was Sergeant of the Pantry to four Tudor monarchs. He fathered 19 children by his first wife and a couple more by his second. (Spare a thought for the first Mrs Corbett as you pass by!)

The walk *Pass Nailstone church on your left and walk along Church Road until it bends left. Turn right when you pass Manor Cottage. Keep close to the hedge on your left. Pass the electricity transformer. When the hedge ends keep in the same direction, across the open field, to meet a hedge on your right. Pass the field corner and cross the waymarked stile. The isolated house ahead is Crown Farm, our next*

The River Lin, Bradgate Park.

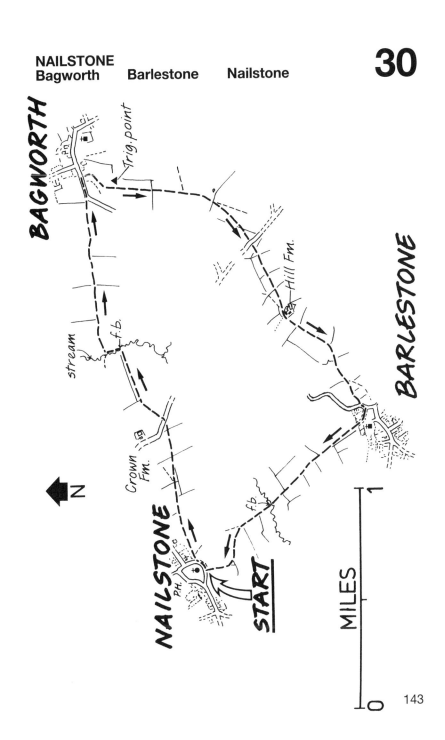

BAGWORTH

Trig. point

Hill Fm.

BARLESTONE

stream

f.b.

N

Crown Fm.

NAILSTONE

P.H.

f.b.

START

MILES

1

0

143

goal. Follow the waymarked path with the hedge on your right, aiming for the right of the building. In the next field, walk with the hedge on your left. Bear right across a small field corner to emerge on the Bagworth road opposite a gate below the Crown farmhouse. Cross the road, go through the gate and continue beside a hedge on your left.

Go downhill to cross the stream and then turn left to the field corner and right to go uphill, still in the same field, beside the hedge on your left.

Continue close to the hedge on the left on a good track, until you join the road. Turn left and walk along the road into Bagworth.

Pass the 30mph sign and the Woodland Trust plaque and then turn right, through a metal gate.At the corner bear right at the waymark post and walk slightly uphill to a stile about halfway along the hedge in front of you. Cross the stile and keep in the same direction parallel with the hedge on your left walking gradually downhill. Pass the new forest plantation on your right, making for the fence gap ahead. In the next field walk close to the left hand hedge, passing a stile on your left.

Near the end of the field move right to cross a stile on the right of an adjoining hedge. Turn left and walk with the hedge on your left to a stile near the corner of the field. Cross onto the Bagworth road.

Turn right along the road and cross the first stile on your left, through a small field to cross the stile ahead. Turn right towards a pylon, keeping in the same direction over two stiles. Pass the protruding corner of the hedge in the next field and walk with the hedge on your right to the farm.

Cross the stile into a small copse to another stile, then pass through the farmyard with a large shed on your right. Cross the stile and walk with the hedge on your right over two fields. In the corner of the second field there are two stiles. Cross the one on the right and follow the green lane which leads to a road in Barlestone.

At the road turn left then right into Washpit Lane. Pass St Giles Close and follow the lane past the church. At Church Farm cross the stile ahead of you, ignoring a stile on your right. Walk down the field parallel with the hedge on your right, aiming for the church spire in the distance. At the end of the field cross the stile at the right of the metal gate and walk with the hedge on your left. Cross the stile and walk with the same hedge on your right. The field slopes down to a stile in the corner. On the far side move slightly left to cross the railed footbridge then walk with the hedge on your right for two fields. Then cross the stile and move left, ignoring the stile on your right. Go uphill to cross

The ruined tower of Ulverscroft Priory.

the stile in the hedge ahead (about 100 yards from the field corner). Walk towards the hedge on the left over a mound to cross a stile in the protruding corner of the next field. Continue with the hedge on your right aiming for the church.

Cross the stile to the right of a bungalow and go up the jitty to Nailstone church.

Steve Westby.

Our foolproofer says: "Gone are the scars of Bagworth's mining history."

BAGWORTH
(Markfield)   Thornton   Bagworth   **31**

How to get there A50 north to Markfield (Field Head roundabout) then left via Thornton and Bagworth.

Car parking Street parking only. The Square, Bagworth.

Public transport There is a regular hourly bus service from St Margaret's bus station to Bagworth (at present Route 254). Ring Busline.

Map Pathfinder 894 (SK40/50) Leicester (West) and Market Bosworth.

Route Undulating ground over a mixture of meadow and arable land. The waymarking is good and the route not difficult to follow.

Mileage 5 miles which can be shortened to 2 and a half miles.

The outward and inward sections of the walk meet at a stile close to Thornton reservoir. At this point you could omit the (uphill) section to the motorway and shorten the walk to 2 and a half miles. The walk can also be varied by adding a very pleasant 2 mile walk round Thornton reservoir.

Refreshment Pubs in Thornton and Markfield.

Items of interest Bagworth, a former mining village.
Thornton reservoir.
Ashley's Wood, recently planted with 3,000 poplar trees as part of the National Forest
Bagworth Park was the site of a great house planned to equal Kirby Muxloe and Ashby Castle, built for William Lord Hastings in the time of Richard III.
Leicester to Swannington railway line, opened by Stephenson in 1832, the first public railway in the Midlands (and now re-opened as the Ivanhoe line.) The Bagworth Incline, where Stephenson's trains were

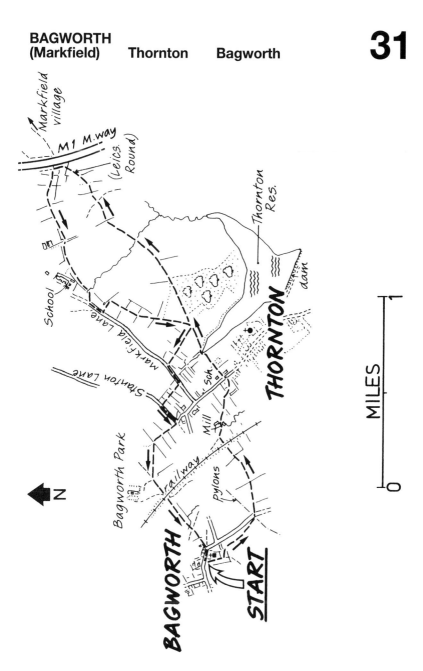

Typical Charnwood countryside near Ulverscroft.

pulled up the hill by an extra engine at the top is now a lovely, quiet, hedged track.

The walk *From Main Street, The Square, in Bagworth cross into Church Hill. The little church is well hidden at the top of Church Hill. Keep to the right of the churchyard and walk close to the hedge on your left. Turn left when you are about halfway along the field. Cross the graveyard, passing the church over to your left. Make for the far right corner of the field and continue in the same direction, walking diagonally downhill (in a field planted by the Woodland Trust) to meet the road where it crosses under the pylon lines.*

Cross the road and continue on the wide green track (past the former site of Little Bagworth on your right). Thornton village lies on the hill ahead. The needle point church spire soon comes into view, slightly to your right. Keep the hedge on your left and follow the enclosed track. When you come to an open field (where hedges have been removed) continue in the same direction to the hedge opposite.

Once over the small ridge you can see stretching along the valley, the old railway line.

Cross into the corner of the field where the hedge juts out and walk downhill close to the hedge on your right. Cross up over the railway line and down to cross the farm road. Continue in the same direction, still with the hedge on your right. Turn right and walk close to the stream on your left. Cross the footbridge over the stream and the mill race and swing left to walk past Thornton Mill, over the cobbles and past the old millstones set in the lane. (The lane leads straight up to Main Street, Thornton, but our path turns off the lane after a few yards.) Turn right at the stile and cross the field going slightly left to enter a small spinney. Turn left through the spinney and then right. Ignore a roadway on your left and join Hawthorn Drive. Walk past the houses to meet Main Street, opposite Thornton primary school.

Our route goes straight ahead, but Thornton village is worth a stop. There are two pubs, both serving food, a shop and buses to Leicester and Coalville. The beautiful church lies to your right. A very small detour takes you past the church, where you can go down to the reservoir and turn left on the reservoir path.

You are now approaching the Charnwood Forest area, and the hills get steeper!

From Thornton Main Street take the path by the school which leads straight down to the reservoir.

The woodland approach to Beacon Hill.

There are fine views here. To your left lies Stanton under Bardon and the half-quarried Bardon Hill. Ahead is the Charnwood Forest area, beyond the beautiful Thornton reservoir.

Turn left along the perimeter path and swing right, round the narrow end of the reservoir. Go through the kissing gate on your left and walk uphill with the hedge on your left at first. Cross into the corner of the field on your left and then go uphill to pass the wood on your right.

From the top of the hill Markfield church can be seen ahead, beside the rocky outcrops of Altar Rocks. The motorway which cuts through Charnwood lies ahead .

Go downhill towards the motorway, with the hedge on your right. Continue in the same direction downhill with the hedge on your left. Go uphill in the same direction. (Do not follow the track to the left!) Make for the big tree on the hill. Descend steeply through the spinney, cross the footbridge and go up to the far right arrow-head corner of the big field. (Look back to see Thornton reservoir in the valley.) Continue cutting across the corners of the next two fields. Turn left to walk beside the motorway on your right.

(TO REACH MARKFIELD village turn right through the kissing gate and go under the motorway bridge. Follow the concrete farm road up into Markfield, emerging near the Bulls Head pub.)

IF YOU DO NOT WISH TO GO INTO MARKFIELD turn left when you reach the motorway bridge and go up a concrete road and over a stile. Walk close to the hedge on your right and cross into another field using a stile in a holly hedge. Keep close to the hedge on the right in this field and the next and exit via the right hand corner into a farm lane. Turn right and then left at a farm gate into the playing field of South Charnwood High School.

Follow the right hand hedge and cross the stile in the corner and continue with the hedge still on your right. Cross the (broken) stile and join the field road. Turn right and walk to Markfield Lane.

Turn left towards Thornton and after about 100m turn left into Ashley's Wood. Keep the hedge on your left and go through the gateway in the hedge. Turn right and walk to the end of the wood, keeping the hedge on your right. In the next field Thornton church can be clearly seen ahead. Aim for it, going downhill close to the right hand hedge. In the next field continue downhill to the far left corner. Turn left into one field and then right into another. The field path takes a line just to the right of Thornton church spire.

Charnwood hill country from Beacon Hill.

Cross the stile onto the Leicestershire Round footpath and turn right and immediately right again to go over the stile onto a farm track and on to Markfield Lane. Turn left and then cross the stile on your right. Cross the field keeping close to the brook. (The waymarks are on the right of the brook.). Cross a series of stiles to Stanton Lane. Turn left and walk uphill to the north end of Thornton. At the top of the hill, just before the road turns left, turn right onto the footpath. Follow this path round the left edge of the field to reach a waymark post.

At this point Bagworth village is visible on the hill ahead.

Cross the stile into the next field and walk diagonally downhill to the waymark post. Continue in the same direction into the plantation for about 20 paces to the stile. Two paths cross here. Take the left path and go towards a railway arch. Pass through the arch and turn right immediately to go through the kissing gate. Head uphill towards a clump of trees hiding Bagworth church. Cross the stile and continue uphill. When the slope eases go towards the wrought iron kissing gate and then into Bagworth village. Turn right to reach The Square, where the walk began.

Clive Fennell: "Perhaps a word of warning is called for! There are about 20 stiles, some in need of repair. Some fields may be ploughed. Near the M1 hollow the traffic fumes could be very irritating to sensitive nostrils."

MARKFIELD
Newtown Linford   Markfield

32

How to get there A50 north from Leicester.

Car parking in Markfield on the main street. There is a Pay and Display car park in Bradgate Park, for those wishing to start from Newtown Linford.

Public transport There is quite a good bus service to both villages. Ring Busline for details.

Map Pathfinder 874 (SK41/51) Loughborough (South).

Route Hilly, wooded countryside. Well waymarked paths. Lovely views of Charnwood at all seasons.

Mileage 3 miles.

Refreshment The pub and cafes in Newtown Linford serve excellent food.
Shops and various pubs in Markfield.

NEWTON LINFORD

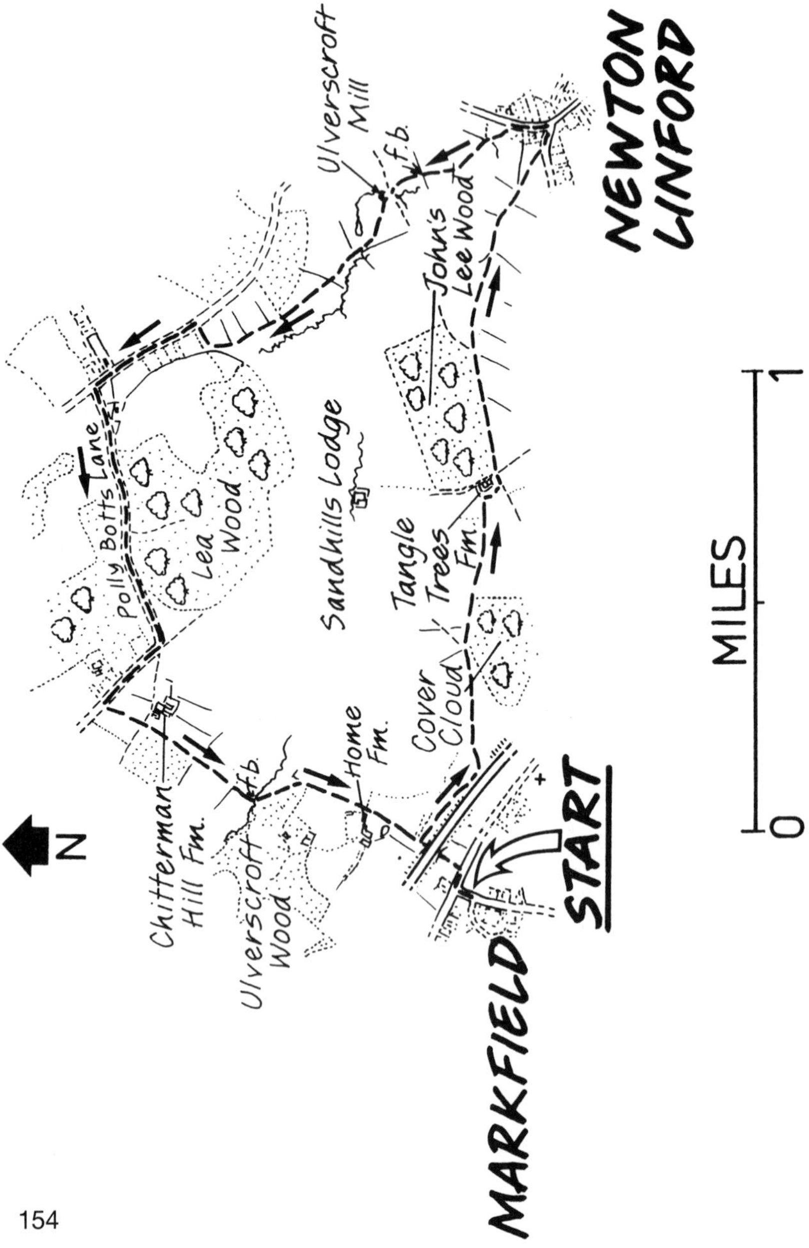

Ulverscroft Mill

F.b.

John's Lee Wood

Polly Botts Lane

Sandhills Lodge

Lea Wood

Tangle Trees Fm.

Cover Cloud

Home Fm.

F.b.

Chitterman Hill Fm.

Ulverscroft Wood

START

MARKFIELD

N

MILES

1

0

Old John, Leicestershire's famous folly built in 1784 on the site of an old mill.

Items of interest Markfield has an interesting mixture of buildings. It is a gateway to the Forest. The Altar Rocks were donated to the public. Newtown Linford is a charming village with thatched cottages.

———————————————————————

The walk *From the top of Main Street, Markfield, take the right hand fork, past the No Entry sign. Turn right along the Leicester Road and turn left at the footpath sign near the bus shelter. Follow the metalled subway under the A50 dual carriageway. Turn left and then immediately right, to walk along the sloping bank close to the hedgerow beside the main A50 road, on your right. Just before the Reduce Speed Now sign, fork left and go down the short slope with a hedge on your left. Cross the stile and go down to the right hand corner of the field.*

Cross a double stile with a slate bridge over the stream. The next field is a large one. Pass the left corner of Cover Cloud wood and continue with the hedge on your right in the next field. Cross the stile on your right and go over the concrete bridge and stile. Turn left to continue in the same direction, with the hedge now on your left.

Tangle Trees farmhouse is ahead. Move right to reach the stile to the right of the house. Go over the stile and cross the drive. Keep the hedge on your right. Pass the house and outbuildings on your left and continue in the same direction to pass John's Lee Wood on your left.

When this track bears to the left, after about 500 yards, aim for the stile in the hedge straight ahead across the field corner. In the next field the hedge is on your left. Cross the stiles and the footbridge and continue in the same direction across the open field. Keep in the same direction, close to the hedge on your right in the first field (cross the footbridge) and on your left in the second.

In the open field continue downhill towards the road. At the road (Markfield Lane) turn left to the road junction, where we turn left. (Bradgate Park entrance lies three quarters of a mile along the road to your right, through the pretty village of Newtown Linford.)

From the Newtown Linford junction with Markfield Lane, turn left and walk along Main Street. Turn left opposite the Johnscliffe Hotel and follow the footpath sign past cottages on your left. Cross the stile and move slightly left as you cross the field, with the tree- lined brook over to your left. Cross the little stone bridge and the waymarked fence and go straight across the next field to the gap in the hedge and continue in the third, small field, to the waymarked fence in the far left corner Cross the footbridge and turn left along a track signposted to Markfield.

A welcome sight at the end of every walk.

Pass on your right the ruined Ulverscroft Mill and turn immediately right to go up the steep bank close to the ruins on your right. Cross the fence and follow the signs to Ulverscroft, going diagonally left. Cross the footbridge over the stream and go over the farm track. Do not swing left but keep the hedge and stream on your left. Cross one footplank and then make your way diagonally right uphill to reach the waymarked stile.

In the next, narrow, field make your way up to the far right top corner. Join a green hedged lane and swing right to go uphill to meet the Ulverscroft Lane. Turn left and walk along the road for about a quarter of a mile and then turn left again to walk along Polly Botts Lane. This quiet country road rises steadily between Lea Wood and Stoneywell Wood and eventually bends right to reach the lovely old houses of Lea Cottage and Stoneywell. Here there is a welcome seat with fine views over the Chitterman Hills.

Cross the waymarked stile on your left, opposite the seat and go downhill close to a drystone wall on your right. Keep in the same direction, crossing the rather awkward stiles. Cross the drive to Chitterman Hills farm and continue with a hedge on your left. As you approach the bottom of the field move slightly right to cross the fence to the right of the farm gate. Continue along the narrow hedged path and cross the pretty bridge over the delightful brook. The path curves left between barbed wire fences and climbs the hill beside Ulverscroft Wood. It continues as a hedged track and meets the bank of the A50 road. Swing right, up the bank and then go under the tunnel of the road to meet the Leicester Road, Markfield, where the walk began.

Bill Ibbs. "In such beautiful countryside, urban areas seem a million miles away."

158

OTHER LOCAL WALKING GUIDES FROM CORDEE

Walking in Charnwood Heather MacDermid

A guide for anyone wanting to explore the footpaths of Charnwood Forest. It contains a wealth of local knowledge and enthusiasm for the area, the countryside and its past secrets.

ISBN 1 871890 18 7   £4.95

The Charnwood Round Heather MacDermid

A map / guide to the 33 mile footpath circuit of Charnwood Forest. A challenge walk with a difference; to be undertaken as one long walk or divided into four easy stages, by using the short cuts that are fully described.

ISBN 1 871890 12 8   £2.95